LIVING THE HIGH LIFE

Living the High Life

HOW SMART CO-OP AND CONDO OWNERS
PROTECT THEMSELVES AND THEIR INVESTMENT

Tina Larsson, LEED Green Associate

Foreword by Mark J. Foley

CLEARSIGHT
BOOKS

Raleigh, North Carolina

Copyright 2022 Tina Larsson
All rights reserved. Copying or use of this material without express written consent by author is prohibited by law.

ISBN paperback: 978-1-945209-36-9
ISBN ebook: 978-1-945209-37-6
Library of Congress Control Number: 2022917669

Published by Clear Sight Books, Raleigh, North Carolina

CONTENTS

Foreword	vii
Introduction	1

Part One — What It Means to Live in a Co-op or Condo

Chapter 1	The Basics of Co-ops and Condos	9
Chapter 2	The Many Co-op and Condo Documents	21

Part Two — Understanding Your Board

Chapter 3	Co-op and Condo Board Basics	43
Chapter 4	Becoming a Board Member—and Why You Should	57
Chapter 5	How to Know Your Board Is Alive and Well	73

Part Three — The Board's Major Areas of Responsibility

Chapter 6	Safety First	101
Chapter 7	Finances	113
Chapter 8	Quality of Life	133
Chapter 9	Sustainability and Energy Efficiency	147

Conclusion	Focus on the Future	163
Acknowledgments		171

FOREWORD

RESIDENTIAL BUILDINGS ARE, in effect, small businesses, and to be successful they need to be run as efficiently as possible. If you are a new co-op or condo board member, you are likely stepping into a role for which you have limited, if any, previous experience. Unfortunately, the business can't wait for you to get up to speed; you need to hit the ground running, as you have an enormous responsibility to the building itself, as well as to each individual owner. In addition to maintaining the safe operation of the building and its component systems, you and your fellow board members will be acting with fiduciary responsibility, which can have legal implications.

While this may seem like a daunting task, it can be extremely rewarding. As a board member, you can have a direct (and hopefully positive) influence on your neighbors' quality of life, and indeed their overall net worth, as one's home is often their largest single asset. Fortunately, you now have a helpful guide that includes concrete steps and plans for implementation.

Whether you are an experienced board member or a complete novice, this informative, engaging book can serve as your go-to source for historical context surrounding the unique residential building environment in New York City, with helpful guidance for overseeing a building's safety and financial well-being regardless of location.

Mark J. Foley
Co-founder, The Folson Group

INTRODUCTION

"Without a sense of caring, there can be no sense of community."

—Anthony D'Angelo

At approximately 1:22 A.M. on June 24, 2021, in the small beachfront town of Surfside, Florida, a large section of the Champlain Towers South condominium building collapsed, resulting in the deaths of ninety-eight people. The tragic event is tied with the 1922 collapse of the Knickerbocker Theater as the third-deadliest structural engineering failure in United States history. While the heartbreaking catastrophe in Surfside is still under investigation and the ultimate cause may take years to determine, the devastation raises many questions, including who might have been at fault and whether the disaster could have been prevented.

Built in 1981, the Champlain Towers South building was due for its forty-year recertification, a requirement that was enacted in response to the 1974 collapse of a rooftop parking lot in Miami that killed seven people. In 2018, during the initial phase of the recertification process, the unsafe conditions at Champlain Towers South became evident when an engineering inspection revealed that the waterproofing layer of the pool deck on top of the underground parking garage had been built without a slant, causing water to collect and damage the concrete structure. The damage was going to cost millions to fix, and, in fact, a $15 million remedial program had been approved. At the time of the collapse, however, no structural repairs had yet begun, due in part to mounting concerns over the building's stability and whether it was sound enough to withstand the repair without its structural integrity being compromised further.

While investigation into the collapse continues, it seems clear that from the start the structure was dangerously flawed. The developer had seemingly taken many shortcuts, including the use of supporting columns too narrow to withstand the load and not enough rebar (the steel reinforcing bar used inside the concrete). But did the engineer who conducted the 2018 inspection notify the condo board and the Miami-Dade County building authorities of the urgency of the matter? Suppose the condo board members were aware that repairs were needed. Could any of them have predicted the consequences as they discussed the plans and costs in the months leading up to the collapse?[1]

It's important to remember that co-op and condo board members are volunteers, and that in most cases, other than the officers, members have no defined functions or responsibilities. No matter who you are in life and business, few of us possess the knowledge or experience to make multimillion-dollar decisions regarding the structural safety of a multistory residential building.

In New York City, where I live, there was a huge building boom in the early 1900s lasting until the Great Depression in the 1930s, so many buildings have withstood more than a century of wear and tear. These pre-war structures are aging, right along with their systems. The steel and concrete in these buildings typically date back to the original structure. The electrical wiring; water,

---

[1] I want to note the *Miami Herald* did stellar investigative reporting on this case.

sewer, and heating pipes; and mechanical systems like elevators and boilers are also likely to date back to the original construction. Many buildings have not been adequately maintained over the decades and increasingly require extensive repairs to keep them safe.

WHO THIS BOOK IS FOR

This book is a resource for co-op and condo owners and their board members. I am writing it to inspire and motivate you to take an active role in shaping the destiny of what is likely your largest investment: your primary home. My hope is that this book will guide you to be an invaluable volunteer and fiduciary as you work to make your own home and your neighbors' homes safer, more sustainable, and more affordable.

Living the High Life addresses some of the most common issues that apartment and building owners face, and the solutions that have proven most effective and affordable. This book also offers valuable tools and tips that can be used to prepare, organize, execute, and even fund upcoming building projects. My goal is to provide you with the resources you need to be a more effective co-op or condo board member or owner.

WHY LISTEN TO ME

I co-founded The Folson Group after working for years as an investment advisor and business analyst, first with an investment advisory firm and then with my husband, Mark Foley, in our own firm. Mark also has a background in finance, and for many years things went quite well. We grew our firm and assets, clients were happy, and we felt great—until the financial crisis hit in 2008. Right after the crash, as we were still recovering, our co-op board sent us their annual letter, which we received on Christmas Eve. The letter informed us that our maintenance fees would be increasing by 5 percent. (Merry Christmas to us!) The increase itself wasn't necessarily alarming, but the fact that it was a 5 percent increase for the tenth year in a row during a noninflationary period made it problematic.

As business analysts who have a good grasp of economics and inflation, we recognized this pattern didn't make sense. By way of background, co-ops and condos are typically run with no profits. During the annual budgeting process, the board estimates all the costs for the year and passes them on to the owners via regular association dues or special assessments. To put it plainly, if your dues increase by 5 percent, it should be only because the building's expenses have also risen by 5 percent.

That's when I told my husband we needed to run for the board to end the unreasonable increases, or else we would need to sell and move. We started talking with some of our neighbors and found that they shared our concerns. We formed a group with three other owners who were willing to step up and nominate themselves to the board. As our building allowed for only one board member per apartment, my husband was the nominee from ours.

All our nominees were elected to the board, and my husband became board president. The new board appointed me to use my analytical skills and head the finance committee. As a general business analyst in my professional life, I simply applied my skills to a different industry. I researched and educated myself on how co-op and condo boards worked and how buildings were run. I also gathered data from comparable buildings by attending open houses in those buildings and reviewing the financial statements from their real estate brokers.

I got to work compiling a benchmark report of hundreds of expense line items for twenty buildings. (Our data has since expanded to encompass 200-plus buildings.) Armed with relevant data, and with the support of the new board, I made some telephone calls, eliminated some services, and got competitive bids on others. Over the first three years, we successfully saved the building $340,000! To this day, with Mark at the helm as president, the board has been able to avoid increasing maintenance fees for eight out of ten years.

At The Folson Group, our strength is helping co-op and condo boards run their building like a business. Our experience working with dozens of buildings, boards, and projects has allowed us to grow and perfect our proprietary benchmarks to enable even more solutions and greater savings. Now you as a reader don't have to tackle this challenge on your own. You can do it with our help and guidance.

WHAT TO EXPECT FROM THIS BOOK

This book is designed for co-op and condo owners, co-op and condo board members, and those considering co-op or condo ownership. We lay out the benefits and challenges, problems and solutions, in simple, straightforward language—no legalese here, just helpful perspective.

In Part One, we look at what it means to live in a co-op or condo, and we delve into the various documents involved.

In Part Two, we examine the role of the board. What are the board members' responsibilities, who supports them, and how do you know if they are functioning properly?

Finally, in Part Three, we discuss some of the major focus areas for a co-op or condo and its board, from safety to sustainability and finances to fun.

Bonus: This book is accompanied by a free downloadable tool kit that includes samples, checklists, and templates you can use to develop short-term and long-term plans for your building's success and safety. To download it, use the QR code below or visit https://www.thefolsongroup.com/book.

At The Folson Group, we are passionate about helping every New York City co-op and condo owner live in a safer, more sustainable, and more affordable building. And while we primarily serve co-op and condo boards in New York City and its boroughs, we know these concerns are universal. So, whether your building is in Los Angeles, Chicago, Fort Lauderdale, or elsewhere in the country, if you own your apartment, this book is for you.

PART ONE

WHAT IT MEANS TO LIVE IN A CO-OP OR CONDO

> *"The greatness of a community is most accurately measured by the compassionate actions of its members."*
>
> —Coretta Scott King

IN PART ONE, WE TAKE A LOOK at the similarities and differences between co-ops and condos and then we dig into the documents that go along with co-op and condo ownership.

■ ■ ■

CHAPTER 1

THE BASICS OF CO-OPS AND CONDOS

"Risk comes from not knowing what you're doing."

—Warren Buffett

IMAGINE THIS: You have just bought an apartment. (Congratulations!) If you're like most people, you love your apartment, especially when it's your first. There is something special about transitioning from renting from a landlord to buying your own apartment.

You have gone through the steps of saving enough for the down payment, working with a mortgage broker and maybe even a credit repair specialist, and securing the services of an excellent real estate broker. You have put in the time to look at what feels like *way* too many apartments. Along the way, it's possible you were turned down by the condo board at one of your favorite move-in-ready apartments, or perhaps you found a move-in-ready dream apartment elsewhere, only to be outbid by a cash buyer. The journey to homeownership isn't always smooth sailing, but you made it.

If you're like many people, you may have found it difficult to envision turning your new apartment into the beautiful space you saw in the pages of *Architectural Digest*, so you decided to work with an interior designer. If you needed to move walls or gas lines, you worked with an architect who filed permits and completed the co-op's or condo's required alteration agreement. You worked with any number of contractors, who each gave you a timeline and a budget. (And you likely found that the construction took twice as long and cost twice as much as you had initially hoped.) Along the way, you paid various fees to the property management firm and the building. Still, you persevered through the renovations, the move-in, and the furnishing of the rooms—transforming it from just any apartment into your own unique space.

Then one day you get a notice in the mail from the board stating that you are not allowed to use your own terrace! The first thing that goes through your mind is probably the fact that there are steps and a door leading to the terrace—how could they stop you from using it? What does the notice mean, exactly? It says that the board will "revoke your proprietary lease" if you do not remove the furniture and planters you used to decorate your terrace.

In a nutshell, having your proprietary lease revoked means you would have to move. Whether you would be able to sell your apartment or not probably depends on the board, and the language around this can be a bit ambiguous.

How could this even happen? And how might you have prevented it in the first place?

Situations like this are not at all uncommon and highlight the importance of understanding what it means to live in a co-op or condominium and the need to be aware of the various rules and restrictions all owners are bound by.

THE MAJOR DIFFERENCES

I was first introduced to these two forms of homeownership—co-ops and condos—when my husband and I began apartment hunting in New York City. Although my husband was already aware of the differences, I was not. I grew up in Sweden and only moved to the US in 1994; there were many things for me to learn that those who had grown up in the US already knew. (I remember once discussing investments with my boss and the Kellogg's brand was mentioned. I had no idea they made Corn Flakes, a product quite familiar to most Americans, so you can imagine how much learning was in store for me when it came to co-ops and condos.)

My husband and I had rented apartments for many years, separately and together. We were told that it was best to buy a condo because the rules were more relaxed, and the down payment was only 10 percent. Well, as you can imagine, it isn't quite that simple.

Co-ops and condos are similar in that residents live in separate apartments with shared common areas (hallways, lobby, roof terrace, community room, fitness center), but they have different rules and regulations, and while both are nonprofit corporations (or other legal business entities), their structure is different.

Ownership. The key difference between co-ops and condos is in who holds the deed or land lease for the housing. In a *condominium*, or *condo*, the individual condo owner holds the deed or land lease directly, just as one might own a single-family home.

In a *co-operative*, or *co-op* (sometimes *coop*), residents own shares in a corporation that owns the deed or land lease. Each shareholder has one apartment assigned to them through a proprietary lease. Each apartment has a certain number of shares allocated to it, often based on the size of the apartment and the floor where it is located. When you buy your apartment, the shareholder certificate will state the number of shares allocated to your apartment. The offering plan, a document that accompanies the purchase of a co-op apartment, is a valuable reference document that contains a list showing each apartment with its number of shares, along with the total number of shares in the corporation. (We'll cover more about this document later.)

Monthly Fees. In both housing arrangements, owners make monthly payments for shared expenses for things like heating, staff, and elevators. In a co-op, the monthly payment is known as *maintenance*, or *maintenance fees*; in a condo, the owner pays what is called *common charges* (often abbreviated *CC*).

Real Estate Taxes. In a co-op, because the corporation owns the deed or land lease, maintenance fees include real estate taxes. In a condo, individual owners pay real estate taxes directly.

Mortgage. In co-ops, there is typically an underlying mortgage; that is, the corporation takes out a mortgage against the deed. The mortgage interest payments are tax-deductible for the owners on a per-share basis. A CPA who is hired by the co-op board to conduct an annual audit provides a record of interest payments to each owner via an annual letter. Additionally, the apartment owners may have individual mortgages.

In a condo, the only property that the corporation is likely to own is the resident manager's apartment, so that is the only property that the corporation can mortgage. Residents themselves hold individual mortgages to their respective apartments.

Down Payment. Another way that co-ops and condos differ is the required down payment when individual purchasers take out a mortgage. Although this varies from building to building, most co-ops require a 20 to 25 percent down payment, whereas many condos require only a 10 percent down payment. For both co-ops and condos, the board may change the percentage required for the down payment if they desire, as long as the bylaws give them that authority.

Why do co-ops typically require a larger down payment than condos do? It all comes down to the risk assumed by the lender. In a condo, the bank lends the money directly to the buyer through the mortgage. If a condo owner is in arrears and doesn't make the mortgage payments, the bank has this information directly and bears the risk of a mortgage default. Co-op owners, on the other hand, are all part of the cooperative corporation and jointly bear the risk of a neighbor's default. By requiring a larger down payment, a co-op ensures that the remaining mortgage amount is a lower percentage of the overall amount and therefore a lesser risk. Also, in theory, a buyer who can afford a larger down payment may be considered less likely to be at risk of default. This also explains why co-ops demand more detailed financial information in board package applications. In some more exclusive (and more expensive) buildings, a 50 percent down payment may be required. It is not unusual to see a $20 million co-op on Park Avenue require the entire payment in cash!

Ability to Sublet. The primary factor that attracts investors to condos is that owners can freely sublet, meaning they are allowed to rent their apartment to someone else without restriction. As with rental buildings, investors often rent out their apartments on day one, and may never actually live there themselves. The result is that condos often have more of a "revolving door" feel than co-ops, where owners must often live in the apartment for two years before they can even *apply* to sublet. As it turns out, condos are priced at a premium for that same reason. In most co-ops, the admissions policy states how frequently owners may sublet and for how long. It is not uncommon for co-op owners to be limited to subletting for no more than two consecutive years, and often with the added stipulation that the sublet not occur more frequently than once every five to ten years.

Which type of apartment is right for you? If you like owning your own apartment and being subject to fewer rules and regulations, then a condo is probably a better fit. On the other hand, if you don't mind following the rules set by the co-op board, and you like the idea of owning shares in the building, then a co-op might be a better option. If you're still not sure which one is right for you, I encourage you to speak with a real estate agent. They will be able to give you more information about co-ops and condos in New York City (or whichever location you're considering) and help you make an informed decision about which option is right for you. Table 1 summarizes the major differences between co-ops and condos.

Note: For this book, I am using the terms *cooperative*, *condominium*, and *homeowners' association* (HOA) almost interchangeably, and I use *association* or *corporation* as umbrella terms for all three. I also use the term *owners* or *apartment owners* even though co-op owners are technically owners of shares or shareholders. You may note that some of the content in this book applies to rental apartment buildings, which my company also serves, but some of the topics are also relevant to a homeowner's association with houses or townhomes. While HOA neighborhoods may not have shared boilers, elevators, roofs, façades, and windows, they may have common roads, landscapes, and pools.

Table 1: Summary Comparison of Co-ops and Condos

	CO-OP	CONDO
Technical Name	Housing co-operative or co-operative housing	Condominium
Short Name	Co-op, Coop	Condo
Owners Are	Shareholders in the corporation. Shareholders do not own the physical space; their apartments are assigned through a proprietary lease.	Individual owners. Because individuals own their apartments, it is harder for boards to regulate them.
Monthly Dues/Fees	Maintenance, maintenance fees	Common charges (CC), or HOA fees
Real Estate Taxes	Paid for by the corporation and included in maintenance fees. Included on the building's financial statement, they often account for 40–60% of the total budget.	Directly billed and paid for by the owners. Not included on the building's financial statements.
Mortgage	Underlying mortgage on the entire building, backed by maintenance fees billed to shareholders.	Residents hold individual mortgages on their apartments; association may own/mortgage building manager's apartment.
Down Payment	Typically 20–25% required; as the corporation is shared, a higher down payment helps mitigate risk of default.	Typically 10% required.
Ability to Sublet	Often restricted to minimize resident turnover.	Easier to sublet because units are owned individually.

SUBSETS OF CO-OPS IN NEW YORK

It's worth mentioning that in New York there are two subsets of co-ops that are income-based and have sales price limitations. These co-ops were set up to encourage long-term residency, and they do not generally attract investors because of the limited upside potential in resale price.

Housing Development Fund Corporation co-operatives (HDFCs) are income-restricted and often sales price–restricted as well. In New York City, most HDFCs were formed after the city took over thousands of neglected apartment buildings in the 1970s, fixed them up, and sold them to tenants for nominal amounts with the requirement of turning them into low-income co-ops. According to the NYC Department of Housing Preservation and Development, there are over 1,100 HDFCs, mostly on the Lower East Side, Upper Manhattan, Brooklyn, and South Bronx.

Mitchell-Lama co-operatives were established in 1955. This affordable housing program created income-restricted rentals and limited-equity co-ops, and resulted in about 105,000 apartments. For the rental apartments, the monthly rent is directly tied to the tenant's income. For the co-op apartments, the purchaser invests a nominal amount and when selling, they are entitled only to the amount they paid, plus capital assessments and their mortgage amortization. Any gain beyond what the purchaser is entitled to goes to the co-op corporation upon sale.

Over the years, some co-ops have gone through the complicated process of buying out the Mitchell-Lama mortgages, dissolving the Mitchell-Lama program, and converting the co-op to market rate. Successful conversions include Ruppert Yorkville Towers (1,258 units) and Southbridge Towers (1,650 units). In January 2022, the governor of New York signed a law requiring that to convert Mitchell-Lamas, 80 percent of residents must vote to opt out, up from the previous 67 percent. This law makes it almost impossible to convert Mitchell-Lamas to market rate apartments.

"CONDOPS"

When my husband and I were apartment hunting in 2003, we were told that approximately 20 percent of the apartments in New York City were condos, with the remainder being co-ops. Learning that, although we had decided we preferred a condo, we looked at co-ops as well.

In 2003, online real estate search capabilities were pretty poor, to put it mildly. (The StreetEasy app had not yet taken off.) Determined to find the perfect apartment, we went from open house to open house, Sunday in and Sunday out. An entire year of searching led real estate agents to remember us and refer to us affectionately as "the baseball player and the Swede." Most of the apartments that we walked into were, in our opinion, unlivable. We heard every trick in the book: "looks like Paris," "a townhouse feel," "high ceilings," "spacious," "needs a little TLC," and the list goes on. One apartment didn't even have a kitchen! It came with a cooking plate in what looked like a closet with the door removed. Even though the apartment was well outside the neighborhood we were searching in and did not have the outdoor space that we required, the real estate agent still recommended to us that we buy it immediately, sight unseen, because it was a "steal" and wouldn't last long on the market. Against his advice, we went to view it (of course). Unfortunately, once we saw it, it couldn't be unseen!

We'd viewed more than a hundred apartments and had the spec sheets to prove it. We were getting frustrated.

Then, all at once, we found four apartments—one condo and three co-ops. When it rains, it pours. Our favorite was the largest apartment of them all, which needed more than a little TLC. It needed a gut renovation. Our attorney wasn't able to get the documentation from management to do her due diligence and advised us to withdraw our bid, which we did. At the same time, we were outbid on the other three apartments, at well over asking price. Tired of spending every Sunday apartment hunting, we put in a second offer, at a lower price, on the co-op from which we had previously withdrawn our offer. We ended up buying it—the largest of the four—at a bargain price to boot.

As we went through the purchase process, we found out that our co-op was technically a *condop*, a mixed-use condominium building where at least part of it is owned by a cooperative (thus condo + co-op = "condop"). Our building was and still is marketed as a co-op, but the retail space on the first floor is owned by a commercial owner and shares some of the common elements of the building through a condominium arrangement. Over the years, we have learned that most buildings with commercial space on the first floor are technically condops. Whether for good or bad, it is rare for co-ops to own their building's retail spaces. Of several hundred buildings in my neighborhood, only a handful of co-ops own their commercial spaces.

When we met with the board members of one of these buildings to discuss what we at The Folson Group could offer them, they told us they didn't need our cost-reduction services because the retail pharmacy on the ground floor paid such high rent that they were all set. I am curious how the pandemic impacted them financially, because that commercial space has now been vacant for over two years. Today, that same avenue has more vacant commercial spaces than occupied, so finding a new tenant might be challenging.

MANAGED OR SELF-MANAGED

One more thing to keep in mind: co-ops and condos can be either self-managed or have a property management firm. *Self-managed* simply means the board and superintendent ("super") often do what a property management company would otherwise handle.

The major building management items include bookkeeping, recordkeeping, building code compliance, and managing resident complaints and requests. Additionally, large property management firms typically have a closing department to manage apartment sales, whereas smaller ones may or may not. Table 2 (on the next page) provides a more detailed listing of all the common responsibilities in managing a residential building. A property management company can perform all of them; if you self-manage, you can do them in-house or you can outsource various duties.

At The Folson Group, boards often ask whether we think it wise for their building to hire a property manager. We always recommend that buildings with fewer than forty units be self-managed. First, smaller buildings require less administrative work than larger ones. Second, the cost of a property manager is shared by the apartment owners; it helps to reach a critical mass to make each owner's portion smaller.

Table 2: Summary of Building Management Responsibilities

Bookkeeping	Accounts Payable
	Accounts Receivable
	Bank Reconciliation
Record Keeping	Service Contracts
	Service Renewals
Building Code Compliance	Deadlines
	Notices
	Scheduling
Resident Service	Complaints
	Requests
Closing Department	Buyer Packages
	Closings
Annual Meetings	Coordination
	Communication
	Voting

If the board and super are overwhelmed with handling these items, they may want to consider the many cost-effective services and tools that can help lift the burden off their shoulders. For example, they could hire a virtual bookkeeper to do the bookkeeping.

We'll talk more about the property manager and other key roles in Chapter 3.

CHAPTER 2

THE MANY CO-OP AND CONDO DOCUMENTS

"Knowledge is power. Information is liberating. Education is the premise of progress, in every society, in every family."

—Kofi Annan

RACHEL, A CO-OP OWNER in a large Manhattan building, contacted me and asked why she had received a "yearly report" in the mail. When I asked what the report said, she replied that it was the "2021 Addendum." The report listed quite a few apartments, and her concern was that her apartment was not included on the list.

Co-op corporations and condo associations are regulated entities, and that means they come with many documents. I am not an attorney, so I am not providing legal advice. However, as a generalist in the co-op and condo space, I think it's important to discuss the types of documents you are likely to encounter as a co-op or condo owner and offer my layperson's interpretation of them. I also want to point you to the right sources where you can find the information you need. My hope is that by providing valuable context and sharing real-life examples—using everyday language—I can make it easier for you to navigate these lengthy documents.

OFFERING PLAN

When a building is converted from a rental property into a condo or co-op by the developer or owner, the residents are offered the right to purchase the apartment that they rent and live in. (In New York City, there was a big conversion boom to co-ops in the 1980s;[2] most buildings converted or built in the 1990s and beyond are condos.) Similar to when a company goes public, this sale is done through an *offering plan*, which may also be called the *prospectus*, or the *declaration of covenants, conditions, and restrictions* (CC&Rs). Once the offering plan or prospectus is finalized, it cannot be altered. Any changes must be made through addendums, which is what Rachel had received in the mail and asked me about.

What's in the offering plan? Although this is a brief summary, the following list gives you an idea of what is included among the hundreds of pages of the offering plan:

- The articles of incorporation
- Information about the building, including the developers and original sponsors
- A list of all apartments
- Numbers of shares that are allocated to each apartment, and total shares in the association
- Floor plans, including terraces (this is often where you find each apartment's square footage)
- Board composition, responsibilities, and minimum and maximum number of board members

---

[2] Jonathan Miller, "Change Is the Constant in a Century of New York City Real Estate," Samuel Miller & Associates (https://www.millersamuel.com/files/2012/10/DE100yearsNYC.pdf).

- Staff (this is where you can find whether your building has a 24/7 doorman, concierge, and so on)
- Statement showing the number of apartments or shares that must be bought by individual owners before the co-op or condo conversion is considered complete (at least 50 percent, but it can vary and will be specified)
- Original house rules

Keep reading for more detail on many of these documents...

BYLAWS

Bylaws are the rules written specifically for the co-op, condo, or homeowners' association (HOA). Even if the bylaws are what govern the association, generally speaking, these laws are overruled by local laws, which are overruled by state laws, with federal law superseding them all. (There are some exceptions. An HOA could have stricter rules than the municipality, and they are enforceable if you agreed to them upon purchase of the apartment. For example, in New York City, it is legal to feed the pigeons; however, many associations restrict you from feeding pigeons near or around the building. Details matter, so always check with an attorney for your specific situation, but the general principle of the order of precedence still holds.)

In our consulting, we often see co-op and condo bylaws that are original to the offering plan documents from the 1980s. This is a dangerous situation. Because changes in the law are enacted regularly, the association's bylaws must be updated periodically to reflect those changes. For example, if your building's bylaws are not in compliance with the Fair Housing Act, a federal law, it's time to update them. Additionally, the risk of litigation continues to be a concern for co-op and condo associations. We frequently see bylaws that do not adequately address how to handle lawsuits, which can present significant risk for the co-op or condo, as well as the owners.

Updating the bylaws requires votes by owners, often creating a difficult and lengthy process for boards to undertake. However, to protect the association and its owners, it's something that we regularly recommend.

HOUSE RULES

While the offering plan and bylaws determine the responsibilities and procedures of the co-op or condo board, the *house rules* focus on the day-to-day aspects of how the building operates and the owners' responsibility to comply with the defined policies, procedures, and guidelines.

Our friend Shane was buying a condo and reached out to ask our opinion on the house rules, which he sent along. The house rules raised more than one eyebrow. Prior to this, we had never seen a set of house rules with more than a few pages; this one was 160 pages! Can you imagine living under that much regulation? Chances are, at some point you'd violate some rule and they could "get you" if they wanted to, even for a minor infraction. We didn't bother to read the entire document, but one stipulation was that no one was allowed to move in furniture until they had attended an orientation meeting. Even the military has fewer regulations!

When we bought our own co-op in 2004, we were handed a

green book containing the house rules—the *original* house rules—from 1989. Among the many problems with these extremely out-of-date house rules were incorrect contact information and the prohibition on the use of "velocipedes" in the hallways (which I'm sure most buildings have a huge problem with). At the same time, none of the newer Razor-type scooters or other commonly used vehicles on wheels were even mentioned. There was no pet policy, nor a smoking policy. Not surprisingly, these house rules said nothing about recycling, as that practice was not commonplace in 1989. There was also no mention of how to behave in certain common areas that had been added since the house rules were instituted, and there was no language reflecting the many changes in fire safety codes, which had been tightened up over the years. The board at the time had been talking about updating the house rules for years, and even had a committee dedicated to this, but it was not until my husband and his fellow board members were elected in 2011 that the document was finally updated.

House rules might seem unimportant, but current and well-articulated house rules are an excellent way for co-op and condo boards to ensure that every owner is treated equally. In today's environment where the focus is on equality, this is especially important. Strictly adhering to the house rules protects the board members and the owners against any disputes, whereas not having updated house rules can leave things open to interpretation, which often leads to conflict.

WHAT HOUSE RULES SHOULD INCLUDE

A "one size fits all" approach to house rules is unrealistic, as each property is likely to have unique issues and circumstances.

The needs and priorities for a forty-story, 400-unit condo with many common spaces, a large percentage of sublets, and short-term residents who do not know one another will differ from those living in a four-story, four-unit co-op, all of whom know each other well and have lived close to one another for years. While some condo and co-op buildings have more lenient house rules, others have pages upon pages of strict regulations. Boards need to find a happy medium that will work for most of their owners. It's not the length of the house rules that matters; it's how current and relevant they are to their residents and the building's particular needs.

Whether composed of one lengthy document or many shorter ones, house rules should address the following:

- How to behave in common areas and inside apartments, including noise, garbage disposal, smoking, and so on
- Move-in and move-out policies
- Buying and selling policies, including the financial requirements for buyers and how sellers can have their broker show the apartment during the sales process
- An alteration agreement, including what types of renovations are allowed, the process for getting them approved, and the process for performing them
- Fitness center rules
- Pet policy
- Energy-use policy

No matter which subject the house rule is meant to address, it should always include the following:

- **Compliance:** Statement that the house rule is subject to the bylaws of the corporation as well as local, state, and federal laws

- **Fairness:** The effective date and who must comply
- **Designations:** Definition of what is covered under the house rule
- **Approvals:** The approval process for exceptions or alterations to the rule
- **Responsibilities:** Owners' responsibilities to comply
- **Limits:** Any specific parameters for compliance

UPDATING THE HOUSE RULES

House rules should be reviewed at minimum every few years to ensure that they are up to date and have not fallen out of compliance with either the New York City building regulations or the owners' wishes and best interests. House rules should always be open for review to ensure they still serve their purpose. Consider rules that are never enforced as being similar to laws against jaywalking: if everyone is jaywalking and no one is ever fined, then what is the purpose of the law?

House rules are usually easier to update than, say, bylaws, and can typically be handled in regular board meetings. In my opinion, house rules should be updated frequently to address various issues and problems. Your association's attorney may advise that you have them review updates, but in my nonlegal opinion, incurring legal fees for something that can be changed in a simple meeting is unnecessary. However, do consult your attorney if the changes are significant or if your board is highly risk averse. (Pro tip: If the house rules haven't been updated from their original version in the 1970s or 1980s, significant changes will be needed!)

Of all the documents associated with a homeowner's association, house rules are the ones intended to serve the current needs of the building and its residents. While condo and property management can use house rules to help set the tone for the building, it's important to remember that these rules should be created with the owners in mind.

COMMUNICATING CHANGES TO HOUSE RULES

Owners should be made aware of any revisions to the house rules so that everyone receives equal treatment and there are no surprises. For example, if a new amenity is installed, such as a fitness center or a roof deck, house rules specifically addressing these areas should be implemented and widely distributed. In a fitness center, rules might include wiping down equipment after it's used and using headphones or earbuds to limit ambient noise. As for a roof garden, the most important rules might be that smoking and barbecuing are not allowed, pets are not allowed to do their business there, and, in consideration of those living on the floor below, residents should refrain from bouncing balls or jumping.

We once spoke with a board that had implemented a new house rule pertaining to their alteration agreement. It turned out that after implementation the property manager failed to distribute the updated house rule to all the owners as he had been instructed by the board. As a result of the revised alteration agreement not being distributed, one owner refused to adhere to the new alteration agreement. The board had to shake it off and move on, while ensuring that the alteration agreement was distributed to all owners for future renovations. This is why it is so essential for boards to follow up on their directions to property managers.

REMINDING OWNERS OF HOUSE RULES

Co-op and condo boards and property managers should also be proactive in communicating with owners about any compliance issues with current rules. For example, if there is a problem with noise, the board should instruct the property manager to reach out to all owners to remind them of the house rules.

ANNUAL ADDENDUM

As stated previously, the *annual addendum,* or *amendment*, contains any updates to the offering plan. But what does that really mean? Some context:

When a developer or building owner converts a rental property to a co-op or condo, there are usually some renters who do not want to buy their apartment and also don't want to move. Perhaps they do not have the means to buy the apartment, or they do not think it is a good investment. Or, they don't want the responsibility of ownership and prefer to rent instead. Typically, as long as the renter continues to pay the rent on time and meets any other obligations, they have the right to stay as long as they want. (If they don't pay? It's up to the sponsor, but you can probably guess the most likely outcome.)

Those rental apartments are usually either kept by the developer/owner or sold to a third-party investor; either one is referred to as the *sponsor*. In most cases for affordable housing and HDFCs, the co-op or condo is the sponsor, with the corporation owning the apartments, and this is occasionally the case for market-rate buildings. But as I explained to Rachel when she asked about her addendum and as I have shared with many clients, historically the unsold shares or apartments were sold to one or multiple sponsors, in most cases an outside real estate investment firm.

Each year, the main sponsor provides the annual addendum, or amendment to the offering plan, that states how many apartments they currently own and a list of those apartments. This list also provides the estimated market values of those apartments and how much each unit's rent collection and maintenance costs are. (So Rachel didn't need to worry about her apartment not being listed—because she owned it!) Additionally, the addendum includes audited financial statements and the annual budget, and so on, so the sponsor has to gather that information from the property management company or other relevant parties.

An interesting sidenote: Because many sponsor-owned apartments in older buildings were rent-stabilized, the sponsors had a negative cash flow for decades. My investment experience tells me that they weighed the near-term operating losses against the potential for future appreciation. They knew what they were banking on, and they were spot on. In the late 1980s, Laura, a friend of ours, lived in a gorgeous twelve-room rent-stabilized apartment on the Upper East Side. Laura and her husband were advised by both their attorney and their CPA not to purchase their apartment, as they deemed it a poor investment. You can only imagine how much her apartment would be worth now. Was this poor advice from Laura's attorney and CPA? Probably so, but they might have weighed the monthly dues versus the potential sale price and decided this was their mutual client's best course of action.

Due to life's natural progression, the percentage of sponsor-owned units has gradually declined over the years. During the conversion boom in the 1980s, it was not unusual to see sponsors owning more than 30 percent of the apartments in most buildings, whereas today the percentage is about half that.

DEED

The *deed* is the legal document that transfers the property right.

In a single-family home or a condo, the property owner holds the deed. If the condo unit happens to be in an apartment building, the condo owner gets a deed specifically for their apartment.

In a co-op, the corporation owns the deed. Co-op owners are technically shareholders of the co-op, and their apartments are assigned through a proprietary lease.

Around the time my husband and I and our neighbors staged our "coup" and took over the majority of our co-op board, there were rumors among neighbors about the co-op not owning the land and that it was a land-lease arrangement. Our group asked the long-term sitting board president if the co-op held the land deed. To our surprise, he did not know. He said that it was very complicated and not clear who the owner of the land was.

We spent ten minutes on New York City's Automated City Register Information System (ACRIS) database, located the property record, and confirmed that indeed, the condo owned the deed to the land and is the owner. Convoluted, yes; complicated, no.

A co-op or condo board does not have to have a crackerjack forensic investigator among its ranks, but knowing one's way around the various building documents is undoubtedly helpful in detangling and simplifying the association. So in addition to the deed, I want to offer a basic explanation of the various leases in an apartment building. (Remember I'm not an attorney!)

LAND LEASE

A *lease* is the instrument through which you rent something: an apartment, an office, a home appliance, a car. A *land lease* is an agreement between a landowner and a tenant in which the tenant leases the owner's land. Any lease has many terms and conditions, but for our purposes the most relevant are the agreed-upon price and date of expiration. The land leases that I have seen firsthand have typically been for a term of ninety-nine years, though in a few cases, as few as thirty.

For condo and co-op owners, a land lease is typically bad news. Why? Because even if your association owns the building you live in, someone else owns the land under it. When leasing a car, you can choose to extend, buy out, or cancel the lease agreement and go with a different vendor. When it comes to a land lease, however, you can't just pick up the building and move it.

At some point, the lease's expiration date starts to draw near, and canceling the lease is simply not an option. The only option is to extend. In some rare cases, we have heard of some associations with a land lease that were able to buy the land from the lessor, but since the lessor has such an advantage, they are not often inclined to offer that option. So, as there's no competition, the land-lease building board is stuck with extending the lease at whatever price the lessor decides. The lessor can charge virtually whatever they want, and the lessee's success at mitigating rate hikes depends on their representatives' negotiating skills.

It is impossible to accurately predict the future monthly dues for an apartment in a land-lease building. This creates uncertainty, making an investment too risky and depressing the market value of the apartments. We have seen many land-lease buildings whose owners' monthly fees increased by as much as fivefold (overnight!) and whose property values tanked when the land lease was either renewed or bought out.

Imagine that you are looking for an apartment in New York City, and you glance through listings online. You find an apartment listed for $500 per square foot when most other older buildings are typically selling for double that. Woohoo! Unfortunately, the probability is high that it's a land-lease building.

PROPRIETARY LEASE

A *proprietary lease*, also called an *occupancy agreement*, gives a shareholder in a housing co-operative the right to occupy a particular unit. In a co-op, the deed belongs to the co-operative association, and shareholders or owners are assigned their apartment through the proprietary lease.

A while back, I was contacted by a co-op owner, Julia, who told me that she had received a letter from the co-op board's attorney informing her they would revoke her proprietary lease if she did not remove the furniture and planters from her terrace. When we spoke with the property manager, he told us that it was common practice to send such a letter. How scary is that? Julia had saved her money and found and bought an apartment; this had taken her several years and required lots of planning and difficult decisions. After finally moving in, she put a planter on her terrace, and now she learns that they can take her apartment away from her? How can that be standard practice?

I spoke with Bruce Cholst, a partner at Herrick Feinstein LLP who focuses on co-op and condo law, to get his opinion on this. I asked him if, in this situation, he would advise his clients to threaten to revoke the proprietary lease any time a shareholder does something that the board deems problematic.

Bruce noted, "The unilateral revocation of a proprietary lease by a co-op or condo board without any prior attempt at an amicable resolution of the dispute is not common practice."

As a board member, it's your job to know what is in the governing documents, and it's your job to make sure they reflect the needs and wishes of the owners. If residents violate rules, don't threaten them—just have a conversation with them. If you need to escalate to the property manager or resident manager, do that. And if a rule isn't working for a large number of residents, you may need to revise it.

AMENITY LEASES

Lease agreements can serve as handy tools for managing the amenities in a co-op or condo: fitness center, storage space, and so on. They are a good tool because they are not permanent and canceling them for nonperformance is relatively easy.

Most buildings have at least one person who is either often in arrears or will pay only when they receive a letter with a court date. Of course, this creates stress and wastes valuable time that the board, super, and property manager could spend on more important things. Informing the resident that they are at risk of having the lease for a favorite amenity revoked can be an effective way to motivate them to pay up.

For any amenity lease, the board needs to discuss and write down what the lease covers, and its purpose. (Writing down and thinking about the how and why is always good planning, no matter what area of life.) The lease should include what constitutes nonperformance and have a plan for how to handle it. And the board should ensure the lease is nondiscriminatory and that they enforce it for everyone.

Two common amenity leases are for the fitness center and for storage space.

Fitness Center Lease. A lease agreement is especially convenient for a building's fitness center or gym. For some reason, while most people are well behaved, when there is any misbehavior, it seems to take place on the roof or in the community rooms, pools, or gyms. Having a lease agreement with the owners who use the fitness center is an easy way for boards to enforce appropriate behavior, as they have the option to cancel the deal with anyone who does not follow the rules.

Storage Lease. Storage areas in buildings must be contained to meet fire code requirements. Many buildings used to have loose items in their basement spaces, but over the years, buildings have become more organized and focused on adhering to fire codes. (There's no greater motivator for boards than being fined after a fire inspection.)

Wire storage bins appear to be the most common containers. They are usually numbered and can be owned either by the building or by a company that leases the bins to the building for a set or variable fee. If the building owns the bins, residents typically rent the bins under a storage lease agreement. Although not common, some buildings have one storage space for each apartment, which the apartment owner rents or, in rare cases, owns directly. The storage may be included in the monthly dues or require an additional fee.

Storage leases are a great option for bike storage, even though in many cases there is no physically locked bike storage space. Bike storage is one of those areas that can get out of control if not properly maintained and cleaned out. If your building does not already have a bike storage lease agreement, setting one up (and simultaneously doing a clean sweep) is just part of good housekeeping. Some boards might ask why they should bother charging $100 a year for bike storage. Our sentiment is that owners who never use their bike may not even remember that they have a bike, so a yearly bill serves as a reminder. In the end, they may decide it's not worth $100 to have a bike that's just sitting in the basement collecting dust. Several years after we bought our apartment, the super mentioned something about our bike in the storage room in the basement—only we didn't have a bike. When the super inspected our alleged bike, he found it had the name of the person we bought our apartment from many years prior.

LAUNDRY SERVICE LEASE

One of the most common leases in New York City apartment buildings is the laundry service lease. The co-op or condo leases their space, generally in the basement, to a laundry service provider for a set or variable fee. This lease typically lasts for seven or eight years and includes provision of the laundry equipment and ongoing servicing of that equipment for the duration of the lease agreement. This lease agreement may also include language designating who is responsible (the lessor or the lessee) for keeping the space and equipment up to building code and for paying the utilities that the space and equipment require.

Laundry service agreements often come with small perks, such as laundry carts, folding tables and chairs, and a payment portal. I don't know if you remember the old days when laundry machines were coin operated. (It is probably not a coincidence that one of the largest multifamily laundry service companies is named Coinmach.) As technology advanced, coins were replaced by payment machines that accepted cash and credit cards, which were later replaced by payment apps.

Although a laundry lease is typically long-term to allow for the laundry operator to recoup its investment cost, the lease can almost always be broken in the event of nonperformance.

WIRELESS TOWER LEASE

Depending on your viewpoint, some buildings were either blessed or cursed to have leased out a portion of their roof to a wireless tower company. This lease is intended to make money for the building association (not to provide wireless service). We have seen leases for towers installed in the 1990s that paid in excess of $60,000 per year. That's not a bad deal for co-ops and condos that are otherwise strapped for money to keep their building up to code. Since wireless providers for the most part now have full coverage, high-paying leases are mostly a thing of the past. Now, even in low-coverage areas, we are seeing leases go for barely $6,000 per year.

Additionally, there is a service called Cellrevenue.com that can review the lease and determine whether the cellphone tower lessee should share the co-op or condo's real estate taxes. Since real estate taxes account for approximately half of a co-op's total costs, you can see how this amounts to much more than pocket change.

In a widely covered news story, the co-op at The Leonori building had entered a lease with AT&T in 1992. The lease stipulated the lessee was to install an electric submeter and pay for its own electric use, but initially, as a temporary measure, the cellphone tower was attached to a submeter that supplied the power to the common areas of the building. In 2011, the board hired an energy auditor to comply with New York City energy regulations. During the audit process, the auditor discovered that the cellphone tower was still attached to a submeter that supplied the power to the common areas of the building. The Leonori's co-op board demanded a $750,000 reimbursement from AT&T. We have reviewed many wireless tower leases and have yet to find a situation like The Leonori's; however, considering the number of buildings in New York City, something similar is bound to be discovered at some point.

If your board is considering a wireless lease, or any other lease, be sure to think about what your end goal is and evaluate the risks and rewards. Write up the key points so that they are easy to review with board members. The entire board needs the same understanding before proceeding. Then consult with a qualified attorney to clarify the actual terms of the lease.

■ ■ ■

WORKBOOK RESOURCES

Our free downloadable workbook contains:
- Sample Bylaws
- Sample House Rules
- And more!

To download the workbook, use the QR code below or visit https://www.thefolsongroup.com/book.

PART TWO

UNDERSTANDING YOUR BOARD

"I think anything is possible if you have the mindset and the will and desire to do it and put the time in."

—Roger Clemens

IN PART TWO, WE DESCRIBE the board structure, explain how to become a board member, and give best practices for a well-functioning board.

■ ■ ■

CHAPTER 3

CO-OP AND CONDO BOARD BASICS

> *"Whether you lead a nation, an enterprise, a community, or a family, we are all in the communication business."*
>
> —Robin S. Sharma

HANK HAD JUST BEEN elected to the board when he asked a sitting board member, Bill, what his new responsibilities would entail. Bill replied that serving on the board didn't take a lot of time because "we mostly sit around and don't do anything." Hmm.

When you began working at your first job, you were probably informed about your responsibilities. Even better, you might have inquired about your responsibilities before accepting the position. I bet that if you were offered two positions, where one included a written description of the responsibilities and the other didn't, you would be more inclined to accept the job with the written description. Why is that? Because in any professional role where your work output is measured—and hopefully rewarded—it helps to know what's expected of you. The same principle applies to any organization, and co-op and condo boards are no exception.

In this chapter we lay out the board structure, roles, and responsibilities, as well as what it takes to be a board member and why you should consider accepting that job.

THE BOARD'S STRUCTURE

Co-op and condo boards have varying structures. The association's bylaws define the minimum and maximum number of board members, and three to fifteen members is fairly standard.

Some boards also have committees that focus on a particular issue or project. For instance, if the board wants to renovate the hallways, there may be a design committee outside the board that is committed to moving that project forward. One of the board members often sits on such committees to serve as a liaison between the committee and the board for the duration of the project.

To help the co-op or condo run smoothly, a board must have a strong set of officers, including president, vice president, treasurer, and secretary, with each individual committed to fulfilling the expectations of their office. A minimum of three people must serve in these four required officer roles; occasionally the vice president or treasurer also acts as secretary.

Here are the officers' primary tasks:

Board President
- Leads the board
- Leads the board meetings
- Oversees the day-to-day operations of the building, often together with the property manager

- Is the liaison between the board and the property manager
- Communicates regularly with the property manager or other expert whenever a problem or issue arises
- Signs agreements and contracts
- Authorizes payments, on their own or together with the treasurer

Vice President
- Supports the president if called upon by the president
- Performs the duties of the president in the president's absence
- Serves as president should the president resign

Treasurer
- Reviews and understands the association's financials
- Reports financial status of the association at meetings
- Oversees and budgets the operating and reserve accounts
- Keeps and maintains the association's financial documents
- Oversees deposits, investments, and the preparation of the budgets
- Ensures bills are paid
- Cosigns checks and documents with the president or secretary

Secretary
- Keeps the association's documents
- Records meeting minutes
- Signs or cosigns documents as needed

THE BOARD'S RESPONSIBILITIES

Collectively, a co-op or condo board's primary responsibility is to look after the operations and financial well-being of the association and to make decisions on behalf of the building's owners, with a crucial component being to protect, maintain, and enhance the property values of their building.

Each board member has a fiduciary duty, meaning they must act in the best interest of their fellow building owners, particularly when it comes to financial matters. Some decisions are difficult to make because they involve issues board members may have little or no prior knowledge about and they often cost money. Those costs are passed on to the shareholders as part of their maintenance fees or assessments, so board members must exercise their fiduciary responsibility.

However, while major decisions can be difficult and costly, the risk of *not* acting may be much greater, as indecision can lead to devastating consequences. Though we don't have insight into how much the board at Champlain Towers South knew about the urgent need for structural repairs, one can only imagine the profound regret such a tragedy would bring to those who were close to the situation.

THE PROFESSIONALS SUPPORTING THE BOARD AND THE BUILDING

Lest you worry that the board must do everything itself, let me assure you that there are professionals who help run the building and implement various projects. Some businesses are fairly straightforward, but a building is quite complex. Aside from the regular day-to-day operations, building operators must adhere to a long list of building codes that exist to protect residents, staff, workers, and the community. And in some cities, unions complicate building operations further. Because of this complexity, it typically requires many different vendors who specialize in the various aspects of operating, maintaining, and repairing a building.

Here I'll provide an overview of the primary professionals who support the board and the building so they'll be familiar when we refer to them throughout the book.

PROPERTY MANAGER

The *property management firm* is a third-party vendor hired by the board, or by the sponsor or developer for new construction or conversions. (Recall that some buildings may be self-managed.) Property management firms assign one *property manager* (frequently abbreviated *PM* and sometimes called *managing agent*) and often a team to support each client's building.

While the board governs the association, the property manager runs the day-to-day operations of the building. As we mentioned in Chapter 1, the PM's responsibilities include bookkeeping (including collections and payments), ensuring that the building adheres to all building codes, responding to resident requests, and implementing various board decisions.

The property manager reports to the board but does not have the same fiduciary responsibility the board does; they are simply contracted to act as an agent for the association. As such, the property manager must work within the board's decisions or direction. The property manager may be involved in projects and may gather and provide bids from a variety of service providers, but they aren't the decision-maker and they don't have the same responsibility to look for cost savings that the board members have. Table 3 summarizes the responsibilities of the two parties.

Table 3: Comparison of Board and Property Management Responsibilities

Board	Property Manager
Governs	Manages the day-to-day administrative tasks
Is a fiduciary to the corporation and owners	Under contract to act as an agent for the corporation
Reviews options and renders decisions	Works within the constraints defined by the board
Oversees the implementation of decisions	Provides options (e.g., project bids)
Seeks cost savings	Is not responsible for saving the building money

What sets a great PM apart from a good PM is that a great PM is also a nice person, one who has consummate people skills, is a great communicator, possesses strong project management ability, and is open to change. Unfortunately, it is not unusual for us to hear from board members that they can't get their property manager to perform certain tasks or provide certain documents. Our answer every time: The property manager works for you; if they cannot meet your expectations, it might be time to evaluate your relationship.

A building's assigned property manager can change over time—sometimes often, sometimes rarely—because the PM changes firms, the PM firm reassigns its buildings, the board requests a change, the board selects a different PM firm, or some other reason. One of the largest property management firms in New York has been successfully acquiring other firms for decades. Its success has attracted a great deal of private equity to the industry, and PM firms are being swept up like hotcakes. With more money behind them, these firms can invest in tools and automation to help them operate more efficiently. In the process, as with any other rapid change, co-op and condo boards, residents, and staff may be hurt or helped.

One of our buildings had had the same property management firm since the building was converted to a co-op in the 1980s. Under the leadership of a new board, the property manager was asked to join an in-person meeting at the building. This must have raised a flag for the PM firm, so one of the firm's owners accompanied the PM to the meeting. The new board president met the firm's owner, who said, "The building looks great. I haven't been here since the conversion twenty years ago." Perhaps the owner shouldn't have admitted to being so disengaged that the last time he'd visited the building was two decades prior; this board subsequently switched PM firms.

SUPERINTENDENT

The *superintendent*, often called the *super* and sometimes known as the *resident manager*, reports to the property manager, and often manages similar operational efforts on a smaller scale. The division of labor between them is often a matter of magnitude. For larger projects that require the involvement of engineers and a bidding process, the property manager typically takes the lead. When it comes to emergencies and instant repairs, like getting the boiler up and running again, fixing the light fixture in the mailroom, or unclogging a drain, it's likely the super will take on the task. Similarly, the PM may do the initial legwork for contracting qualified inspectors, but the super will likely schedule the ongoing routine inspections. The super also trains and oversees the rest of the staff, such as doormen, porters, concierges, and other workers.

In our consulting work, we meet a lot of supers, and it's our experience that the super is the glue that makes or breaks a building. When we visit a new client's building, we ask the super for a tour, including the roof, the hallways, any amenity spaces, and the basement and all the systems there. We ask many questions, and the super generally knows their building inside and out. We find most supers to be enthusiastic and accommodating, and it's easy to see they take pride in their building. This sense of ownership is reflected throughout the building, from the most visible common areas to the darkest corners of the basement. (Pro tip: If you provide services that require you to visit different apartment buildings, or even if you're on your own apartment hunt, ask to see the basement. Pay attention to how neat and organized it is. Your findings will say a lot about the super.)

BUILDING STAFF

Beyond a property manager and super, your building likely has a variety of other regular staff, such as doormen, porters, concierges, and maintenance staff.

Most NYC buildings have one door attendant per shift. The attendant opens doors, accepts and delivers packages, and helps residents grab a cab. They also answer residents' top two questions: "How's the weather?" and "Is the mail in yet?" In a building with

24/7 door service, four attendants typically cover all but one of the twenty-one, eight-hour shifts each week, with one of the other staff members covering the remaining eight-hour shift.

Many newer buildings developed or converted in the last twenty years are marketed as luxury buildings and have concierges that do everything from booking Broadway show tickets to making dinner reservations. This means that the building has a concierge in addition to the doorman, which doubles the number of salaries being paid. This additional salary is, of course, passed on to and paid for by the owners. The number of staff is typically part of the original offering documents and can't easily be changed, so when apartment hunting, it's a good idea to ask yourself whether you want to pay for that extra luxury or not.

In smaller buildings, the super often acts as the handyman, doing light repair work, building maintenance, and upkeep. In larger buildings, there is often a designated handyman who is responsible for those types of tasks that the resident manager doesn't have time to perform. Often the handyman or super has a plumber or electrician license, or both, so that they can perform some repair work in those areas.

Porters are the staff members who keep the building clean and tidy, under the direction of the super. They are responsible for taking the garbage out to the curb, handling recycling, sweeping, and cleaning windows and mirrors, hallways, basement corridors, and much more. It is not unusual to see the porter wash the sidewalks in the mornings, polish the brass, and even paint different areas of the building to keep it up to snuff.

Knowing the names of your entire staff and thanking them for their work makes them feel appreciated and goes a long way toward building a great community.

FINANCE PROFESSIONALS

If you have a property management firm, their staff maintain the day-to-day bookkeeping records of the association to make sure that the money is available to meet the association's needs. They will likely use property management software, which is similar to QuickBooks but specific to the property management industry. If your building is self-managed, you could use QuickBooks (or any number of other options) and combine that with hiring a parttime bookkeeper to manage the books.

Additionally, you will need a CPA for two purposes: (1) completing required tax filings, and (2) auditing the association's financial statements. Smaller associations are often not required to audit their financial statements: refer to your offering document to find out whether your association needs to audit its financial statements. In order to conduct audits, the CPA gets the books and records from the property management firm or bookkeeper and verifies the invoices and payments according to a common set of audit principles and rules.

LEGAL PROFESSIONALS

Typical legal matters for an association include routine legal representation, changes to bylaws and other governing documents, contract review, access agreements, American Institute of Architects (AIA) documents and contracts, dispute resolution, mediation, and litigation.

Boards typically engage one attorney who represents the association on an ongoing basis, but they may require the services of more than one attorney, as each may specialize in a particular area of law. If the primary attorney is employed by a large firm, that firm can usually handle all pertinent matters. However, large firms often come with high hourly rates, so the board may opt to engage an attorney from a smaller firm to handle routine legal matters of less significance. A financially savvy board will routinely weigh the complexity and potential risk of various legal matters against their duty (and desire) to make prudent financial decisions on behalf of the association.

ARCHITECTS AND ENGINEERS

For a variety of projects, you will need to engage architects and engineers. A while back, as a condo owner who had been involved with our association board, I was contacted by Mary, a new board member, who called me because she was puzzled why we had two engineers plus an architect on contract.

The easiest way to explain the difference between an engineer and an architect—and to justify the need for both and for more than one in some cases—is to compare them to doctors. An architect is like your primary care physician, a generalist who has basic knowledge across a broad area. An architect is the perfect choice for projects that need the input of a big-picture thinker, a visionary who can provide several general concepts or alternatives so that owners and boards understand their options. An architect typically creates concept drawings, also known as renderings, of a proposed change, such as a new lobby configuration. And just as your primary care physician would recommend you consult a specialist when needed, an architect likewise directs clients to the appropriate specialist, such as an engineer.

Engineers are the specialists who focus on specific requirements within the overall design, such as the HVAC (heating, ventilation, and air-conditioning) system or lighting specifications for the new lobby. Just as you wouldn't visit an orthopedist for an annual physical, you wouldn't go to a mechanical engineer for architectural renderings. There are many types of engineers, each specializing in a specific area and having a basic knowledge of related areas.

Mechanical engineers work on the mechanical systems of a building, including the HVAC system. Other mechanical systems include lighting, sprinklers, standpipes, and elevators. Mechanical engineers are often called upon to lend their expertise to any sustainability efforts that the association undertakes, and they typically perform required inspections, energy audits, and the like.

Structural engineers may specialize in analyzing the building's structure to ensure it is safe. They examine loads, steel, and loadbearing walls, and often oversee large construction projects. For instance, when New York City built the Second Avenue Subway, structural engineers inspected the buildings above and around the planned subway to confirm that they would remain safe as the work took place. During construction, I witnessed firsthand that they placed instruments on the building façades to measure any vibration. In the buildings' basements, engineers placed instruments on every existing visible crack in various spots to measure any changes resulting from the construction. The engineering team monitored those instruments daily, which was comforting, as our windows shook every time the construction dynamite team blasted the solid bedrock below. (I was surprised to learn that those blasts were monitored remotely, as many other aspects of the construction appeared to be less advanced and were instead performed manually.)

Particular projects may require one or more specialists. For example, when you repair the building envelope—the separation of the interior and exterior of a building—you hire an exterior engineer, also called a building envelope engineer. Exterior engineers work on everything related to the exterior of the building: façades, roofs, and windows. These engineers also deal with parking garages, as they are typically built with the same materials as the building. Exterior engineers are the ones who order the sidewalk shed to be installed when they observe unsafe conditions that could potentially harm pedestrians. The exterior engineer is also responsible for drawing up the plans and bid documents for New York City's Façade Inspection Safety Program (FISP).

And when we replace elevators, also known as an "elevator mod" (short for modernization), we typically recommend using an elevator consultant. Many elevator consultants are either mechanical engineers or former qualified elevator mechanics.

OTHER SPECIALISTS

Of course there are many other vendors and specialists who may be involved in servicing your building: plumbers, electricians, HVAC specialists, lighting designers, energy auditors, and on and on. It might seem overwhelming at first to learn what they all do, but just remember: they are all there to help you.

■ ■ ■

WORKBOOK RESOURCES

Our free downloadable workbook contains:
- Sample Meeting Agenda
- Sample Meeting Minutes
- And more!

To download the workbook, use the QR code below or visit https://www.thefolsongroup.com/book.

CHAPTER 4

BECOMING A BOARD MEMBER—AND WHY YOU SHOULD

"Sometimes if you want to see a change for the better, you have to take things into your own hands."

—Clint Eastwood

IN ANY ORGANIZATION, there is good leadership and bad. The same goes for co-op and condo boards.

Remember our first-time owner, Julia, whose decorated terrace prompted a not-so-friendly letter threatening to revoke her proprietary lease? In case you hadn't guessed by now, in my view, the board at Julia's building did not fit the definition of good leadership. Even though the board members' tenure ranged from many years to several decades, they had not educated themselves on the rights of the co-op owner and had no basic knowledge of the co-op's offering plan documents, which clearly stated that Julia's apartment came with a terrace. The board members were hesitant to think for themselves and relied almost entirely on their hired counsel. As icing on the cake, their counsel was not a lawyer who specialized in representing co-op and condo boards; he was a litigator. And remember: a litigator makes more money when there's litigation. If that's not a recipe for failure, I don't know what is.

You might say to yourself, I don't have a terrace, so this won't happen to me. That may be the case, but many other scenarios "happen" to you as a co-op or condo owner.

Your building got a "D" energy efficiency score and it's posted right smack at the lobby entrance. That can't be good for property values. That happened to you.

Your building faces hundreds of thousands of dollars in annual fines because it spits out too much carbon. That happened to you.

Your basement lights are on 24/7/365. That happened to you.

You have one basement room stockpiled with what looks like junk where there could instead be a gym for the residents. That happened to you.

New York real estate prices are among the highest in the country. Every square foot is a highly valued property area. And yet your building is wasting the roof space with . . . nothing. That happened to you.

What can you do to prevent something like this from happening to you? The best way to have a say is to *volunteer for your board*.

Unless the bylaws state otherwise, the board makes decisions on behalf of the entire building. As a passive apartment owner, your influence is limited to voting for the handful of neighbors who get to make those decisions. You may not agree with their decisions, just as you don't always agree with your local or national political representatives. Your board could decide to choose a litigator as its counsel, determine that the lobby doesn't need a paint job, and decide that the basement lights should be on 24/7 despite its being empty 90 percent of the time. Some buildings have a maximum dollar amount the board can approve without requiring a vote from the owners. One of our clients requires that owners must approve any capital improvement work exceeding $25,000, while another requires approval above $100,000. But many bylaws do not address a maximum spending limit at all, which translates to a board with significant power to impact owners' finances.

As an active board member, you play an integral role in making decisions on behalf of your neighbors. It is a gratifying job if done correctly, but remember that serving on the board is an unpaid volunteer position, one that carries the weight of fiduciary responsibility and requires time and effort. Serving on a passive board that takes care of emergencies only can be pretty stressful, but serving on an active, engaged board where members are focused on results can be quite fulfilling. It can also bring a healthy boost to your self-confidence and a sense of belonging, pride, and accomplishment.

QUALITIES THAT MAKE A GREAT BOARD MEMBER

The combination of traits and skills found among board members can make or break a board and its homeowners' association.

Generally, a great board member is one who is:
- Open to change
- Great at building relationships
- Good at communicating (often misconstrued as being a good speaker but in reality is being a great listener)
- Organized

- Ready to make decisions and challenge the status quo
- Action-oriented

The more of these traits each individual board member has, the easier it will be for the board to make sound, well-considered decisions. But not everyone needs all of them. It's okay if each board member has two or three of these traits, as long as when the board comes together, it functions well as a group. Change is difficult for most people, but it's essential if you want to improve your building. When board members are flexible and willing to listen to others and consider a wide range of options, they are likely to find it much easier to make meaningful changes.

Additionally, it's important for the board to have a well-balanced set of relevant skills, and an owner's vocation can also greatly enhance their contribution as a board member. The following professions have proven to be especially beneficial:

- Architect, building engineer, or a contractor who understands buildings and projects.
- Financial professional who understands business. Note that many financial professionals excel in sales, but what's really important is that they understand business at a granular level.
- Business consultant who specializes in operations and efficiency. The individual with this background often understands the importance of bringing in the right professionals to help with each project.
- Project manager, for example, an events coordinator, IT consultant, executive assistant, facilities manager, or anyone else who coordinates projects.
- Business attorney (preferably one who is not a litigator!).

Finally, apartment owners come from diverse communities with different backgrounds, political views, and economic and family circumstances. A board comprising individuals with greater diversity helps ensure the entire community is represented fairly.

THE NOMINATION AND ELECTION PROCESS

Board members are typically elected at the association's *annual general meeting (AGM)*. In the old days, all you had to do was show up at the meeting, and when the board asked, "Do we have any nominations from the floor?" you simply raised your hand. This sounds archaic but is still common practice in many co-op and condo associations.

A better practice is to have a formal nomination process—one that's communicated in advance. At The Folson Group, our opinion is that if someone does not want to put the time and effort into applying for the position, then it's unlikely they would be a valuable addition to the board. The board should set the nomination process well ahead of the annual meeting and announce it to the entire community. You can imagine the chaos it would create if an owner had planned to nominate themselves at the annual meeting and it had not been announced ahead of time that the board had changed the nomination process.

A best practice for nominating board members is to require all nominees to submit their resume, biography, or qualifications and a statement why they should be elected (this document does not necessarily need to look like a formal resume). It is also up to each candidate to write what they feel comfortable sharing with their neighbors. Since a co-op or condo is a homeowners' association, candidates may want to add information such as when they moved in, who lives in the apartment with them, the reason they are running, and the reason they believe their neighbors should vote for them.

This practice demonstrates that the board takes its responsibility seriously, and most importantly, treats the association like a business. They care about the owners enough to present them with qualified candidates. This helps owners make an informed decision about who they want to represent them for the next board term. For co-ops and condos with annual board terms for their members, we recommend that the sitting members submit their biography every year when running, just as new nominees are asked to do, so that all candidates may be considered equally. This will help quell doubt about the legitimacy of the process or the appearance of favoritism toward sitting board members.

(Occasionally a board seat comes open mid-year. In that case, the sitting board can usually assign someone to the seat, though that will depend on the association's bylaws. And when that does happen, we always recommend vetting proposed board members' qualifications just as you would during a regular election.)

At the AGM, the actual election takes place. There are two forms that often come into play during the process: the ballot and proxies.

BALLOT

The *ballot* is an official document used by shareholders or owners to vote on specific actions, such as capital improvement budgets and election of board members. The ballot lists the names of the board nominees. Typically, the ballot will also include a few blank lines where owners can write in the names of those they want to nominate; however, as mentioned earlier, we advise our clients against the common practice of nominating at the meeting. (Could you imagine attending Apple's annual meeting and finding out that they allowed shareholders to nominate themselves to the board at the last minute? As the British would say: not bloody likely!)

PROXY

A *proxy* is a document that legally authorizes someone to cast votes on another person's behalf, like a power of attorney but for elections. (While an attorney told me that a proxy can be written on anything, even a cocktail napkin, I strongly recommend if you give or receive a proxy that you type it up, as you do not want to be in the position of having it disregarded.) Using proxies is customary practice for corporate shareholder meetings where it's impossible for all stock owners to show up in person; those not in attendance can usually vote online or via mail, or they can give their proxy to someone to vote for them. What's important to know is that whoever holds the proxy can vote however they like—which may not be the way the proxy giver intended them to vote.

In co-op and condo associations, it is common for someone running for the board to gather proxies from other residents. Does this seem like a conflict of interest? Yes. Does it still happen? Yes. In the free workbook that accompanies this book, I provide two sample proxies: one that is very short and simply assigns power and one that has space for including your voting preferences—but keep in mind that the person holding the proxy is not bound by them.

OTHER GUIDELINES

The AGM invitation, including instructions for nominations and proxies, needs to be provided to shareholders and owners ten to sixty days prior to the AGM. We'll talk about the AGM more in Chapter 4.

While an association's bylaws spell out its nomination and election process, state laws also give you rights. In New York:

- Co-ops are corporations governed by the New York Business Corporation Law. Article 6[3] addresses everything related to elections, annual meetings, proxies and so on; article 7[4] addresses officers and directors.
- Condos are governed by the New York Condominium Act, Article 9-B.[5]

For legal questions specific to your situation, be sure to consult an attorney.

OUR BOARD STRATEGY

My phone rang, and the polite, well-spoken caller introduced himself as Richard. He explained that he was a co-op owner and was concerned about his increasing fees. He was paying more and more, and yet the building was aging, had not been adequately

---

[3] https://www.nysenate.gov/legislation/laws/BSC/A6
[4] https://www.nysenate.gov/legislation/laws/BSC/A7
[5] https://www.nysenate.gov/legislation/laws/RPP/A9-B

maintained, and needed a lot of repairs. I listened and asked a few follow-up questions. (Believe it or not, I spend a lot of time being a co-op "therapist.")

Richard had lived in his apartment for decades and had seen the building go from well-kept to being in dire need of upgrades. He said the board president ran the show and acted as if he owned the building. At the annual meeting a few weeks prior to his call, Richard and his neighbors had asked the board what the maintenance and repair plans were, but the response was that none were planned.

If I had a nickel for every time we got a call from a co-op or condo owner with nearly this exact same story... Our advice (again): If you want a change, *volunteer for your board*.

But what's a practical way to do that? You've got the nomination and election process information, but how do you go about running in a way that will increase your chance of success?

For optimal results, we do not recommend that you run by yourself. If you are the sole voice seeking change, you risk being voted down and not getting anything accomplished. That's a waste of your time and can result in your job being draining, stressful, and exhausting. Instead, our recommendation is to *run as a group*. This maximizes your chance of having a majority of board votes and being able to get things done.

GET TO KNOW YOUR NEIGHBORS

Start by making a casual acquaintance with some of your neighbors. Once you have built a little rapport, you can switch those conversations from "good morning" and Fido-talk to elevators, installing a roof garden, laundry rooms, or recycling. Without seeming too obvious or nosy, you can quickly figure out your neighbors' feelings about the building, the board, and even individual board members. By listening and letting them talk about their personal and professional lives, you can understand whether they would be ready to roll up their sleeves and make some changes. See Chapter 8 for more on getting to know your neighbors.

MAKE YOUR WISH LIST

Identify specifically what it is you wish to change. What's on your wish list? Do you want a gym, a roof garden? Do you wish the common areas were painted more often? Imagine you live on the top floor of your building and the fifty-year-old elevator is frequently out of service. This annoys you, especially on days you carry home bags of groceries. Not only is the elevator unreliable, but due to its age, it isn't able to accommodate the installation of a mechanical device required by new regulations, so your co-op is fined every quarter. The elevator needs to be replaced.

TALK WITH INCUMBENT BOARD MEMBERS

Speak with existing board members to find out where they stand on the issues important to you, and for now, we suggest you not tell them about your plans to run for the board. Ask a few simple questions related to your wish list: Have you considered adding a gym, or developing a roof garden, or replacing the elevator? See what their responses are, and try to determine how many board members share your wishes and concerns and how many have different priorities (or, worse, have no priorities at all). The number of board members whose views differ from your own is precisely the number you need to gather in your camp to succeed in making a positive change.

GATHER A GROUP OF LIKE-MINDED NEIGHBORS

Speak with your neighbors and find those who have the same wishes as you. Find the neighbors who are interested in adding that gym or garden. If you think the building needs a new elevator, talk to your neighbors on the top floors who likely feel the same way; see if they would be willing to run for the board with you so that this project can finally be addressed.

Keep in mind that everyone does not need to want the same thing for the same reason. If you want to install a roof garden on the unused tar roof, you want a few people with the same end goal, but their reasoning for wanting a roof terrace can be completely different. You might like to read books and would prefer to do that in nature, on a landscaped terrace. Another person might share that they have heard that having a community roof terrace increases the building's property values. Another person might love to garden and would like nothing more than to head the garden committee, pick weeds, and grow herbs. That would make a perfect group of three. The reason is not essential; the wish and goal are.

Once you have your group together, be ready to roll up your sleeves.

MAKE AN ASSESSMENT

Before you finally decide to run, make a logical assessment of the situation.

- Create a list of the apartments in your building, including the names of the residents in each and add a column to track those you think would vote for you (or sign a proxy for you) if you run.
- Consider the skills and qualities described earlier as desirable for great board members. Which can be found on the current board? Which can be found in the like-minded neighbors you've identified? Which do you bring to the table?
- Finally, ask yourself: if your group wins, will you have a good mix of characteristics so that you have an effective board?

Ready? Set. Run!

COMMONLY ASKED QUESTIONS

My friend Sherri told me she was thinking of running for her co-op board. Sherri is a lovely human and very outgoing, so it was no surprise that she has many friends in her building. Many of her neighbors have asked her to run for the board, multiple times. Like many people, she has a job, a family, an energetic puppy, hobbies, community garden obligations, and a couple of charity involvements.

Sherri's question: How do I fit another "thing" into my already busy life?

Her concerns are similar to those of many co-op and condo owners we have spoken with over the years, so I will share a few of the most common questions, along with my solutions and observations.

HOW MUCH WORK IS REQUIRED TO SERVE ON A CO-OP OR CONDO BOARD?

The work required to be a volunteer board member varies. At minimum there are monthly meetings with the associated preparation and follow-up. But in my experience, when you are passionate about something, you generally put more time and effort into it. If you feel strongly about installing a gym in your building's basement, you will work on solutions to make that happen. If you do not care either way about it, you are unlikely to skip your daily meditation to attend a planning meeting about it.

We all have different motivators that will influence the amount of time we are willing to commit: money, recognition, passion, meaning, and curiosity. Do any of these sound like you and your reason for volunteering?

- It personally benefits me and/or the community.
- It will cost me more if we don't do something.
- The building is in such dire straits that unless we undergo massive repairs, it could end in a disaster.
- I want to be involved and give back to my community.
- I always wanted to know what the board members do and how a building is run; how difficult can it be?

To be effective, you do need to commit to a minimum amount of volunteer time, but ultimately you control the maximum.

AS A NEW MEMBER, HOW DO I MAKE MYSELF MOST VALUABLE AND EFFECTIVE?

Start by educating yourself on how buildings are run. That doesn't mean you need to learn every aspect of operating the building. As with other aspects of life, it's easier to understand the topics that interest you or that you are passionate about.

If the elevator is routinely out of service, you're probably more passionate about fixing it if you live on the top floor rather than the second floor. Or suppose you have a cramped studio apartment; you're probably more likely to look into installing more storage bins than the person who just moved into a three-bedroom apartment by herself. If you are passionate about protecting the environment and reducing your carbon footprint, start there, as you'll find ample opportunities to update wasteful practices and improve sustainability.

Engage in a bit of self-discovery by asking yourself what makes you tick when it comes to your building, apartment, or community, and then focus your volunteer efforts in that direction.

HOW DO I MATCH MY STRENGTHS TO MY RESPONSIBILITIES?

What do you enjoy doing in your personal or professional life? If that is something that your co-op needs, spearhead it! If you are passionate about making your building more energy efficient, spearhead your co-op's green initiatives. You already understand and enjoy the topic, and the board and co-op will benefit from your expertise; that's a win-win for everyone.

We often see boards whose members do not use the tools that serve them so well in their professional lives, such as cloud storage for building records or scheduling apps to help them plan meetings. If your professional training or experience has introduced you to useful, innovative tools and practices, please consider sharing them with your fellow board members.

HOW DO I SAY NO (AND LET SOMEONE ELSE VOLUNTEER)?

The beauty of volunteering is that it's precisely that: volunteer. If you're on the board and don't want to plan the holiday party, don't! Ask if another board member will plan it. If no one steps up, send a note to shareholders asking them to volunteer. If there are no volunteers, there will be no party; it's as simple as that.

When owners do volunteer, ask them to suggest boundaries for board approval: suggested date, time, location, theme, and budget. By requiring this simple step, the board ensures the volunteer has done some research before the event, thereby taking the responsibility off the board members' shoulders.

■ ■ ■

WORKBOOK RESOURCES

Our free downloadable workbook contains:
- Sample Proxies
- And more!

To download the workbook, use the QR code below or visit https://www.thefolsongroup.com/book.

CHAPTER 5

HOW TO KNOW YOUR BOARD IS ALIVE AND WELL

> *"If everyone is moving forward together,
> then success takes care of itself."*
>
> —Henry Ford

A HIGH-FUNCTIONING BOARD is critical to the success of a co-op or condo. A board that functions well can provide strong leadership, strategic direction, and oversight. Additionally, a high-functioning board can help the association achieve its goals and objectives. That is, of course, assuming the board *has* goals and objectives. In for-profit businesses, having clear goals and objectives is commonplace, whereas in co-ops and condos, it is unfortunately rather rare. What follows are recommendations to keep your board functioning optimally.

CODE OF ETHICS AND CODE OF CONDUCT

The *code of ethics* and *code of conduct* are documents that lay out general guidelines for how board members are expected to behave, and they provide specific guidance for handling issues like harassment, safety concerns, and conflicts of interest. In your professional life, you may have signed similar documents when you were hired, and some employers require employees to sign them on an annual basis. Yet you would be surprised how many co-op and condo boards do not have these documents.

These codes might seem trivial. The board has so many things to work on, and it can be frustrating to spend time on paperwork and formalities when other, more urgent issues need to be addressed. While I understand, I do not agree with that sentiment. These documents help ensure the integrity of your board, and they can be useful tools when it comes to managing problematic board members.

A well-written document codifies that board members serve in that capacity *only* when in a board meeting. Outside the board meeting, they are simply owners, just like every other owner. Signing and adhering to the codes prevents board members from talking with their neighbors about how they voted against something or didn't agree with the rest of the board's votes. It also discourages them from accepting or demanding favors or special treatment from the staff.

We highly recommend having all board members sign the codes upon adoption and immediately following each year's annual meeting. In our experience, many long-term board members who haven't signed these documents in the past do not want to sign them. Making signatures mandatory for all board members is one way to discourage the holdouts from nominating themselves in the next election; it may even convince them it's time to resign immediately.

MONTHLY MEETINGS

Most co-op and condo boards meet monthly. The monthly meeting is where issues that have accumulated over the month are on the agenda for discussion. All agenda items should be addressed, voted on if appropriate, and documented in the meeting minutes. Should the board run out of time, the remaining agenda items can be tabled to the next monthly meeting, but this should not become a habit.

If the board regularly tables agenda items or if the monthly meetings often exceed sixty minutes each, it might be time to evaluate whether you should meet twice a month or even weekly. During the planning stage of large capital projects, boards can follow the roadmap of successful business owners who have meetings and make decisions more frequently than once per month.

LOCATION

In the "old days," boards used to meet in one of the board members' living rooms, a community room, or a super's office. Nowadays, they primarily meet via Zoom. If you do meet in person, we recommend meeting in the property manager's conference room to get the group's full attention; this setup helps make meetings as effective and efficient as possible.

ATTENDEES

A board quorum, meaning a majority of the board members, including at least two officers, should be present at every monthly meeting. If there are five board members, at least three need to be present, including at least two officers. If there are fifteen board members (the largest board we have seen), a minimum of eight need to be present with at least two officers.

The super or resident manager should also attend board meetings. You would be surprised how often we hear that the super is not invited. Those boards defend their decision by claiming they discuss sensitive information and owners' various "situations," but attendance by a super is necessary to make the meetings as productive as possible. Having the super attend is not only more efficient, but it also makes them feel valued, shows they are a trusted part of the team, and helps give them a sense of ownership.

The property manager and their assistant (if they have one) should attend most but not necessarily all meetings.

MEETING STRUCTURE

Our recommendation is to divide the agenda into three parts. Begin with the super's report, then follow with discussion of any issues that pertain to the super and items that the super will need to act on. Finally, allow the super to leave and finish the meeting with the agenda items that do not relate to the super and may be sensitive in nature (never mind the fact that the building staff usually know *way* more about sensitive or personal information than the board will ever hear). This way, the super, who typically is available 24/7, can leave the meeting early to get back to their family or other activities.

This meeting structure helps alleviate any glitches in communication that tend to occur when the super is not in attendance. If the super is not present at the meeting, then someone else, most likely the property manager, will need to report on the super's behalf. Then, after the meeting, they will need to report back to the super to pass along any questions from the board and convey follow-up actions resulting from decisions the board made during the meeting. Like the game of telephone, this often leads to miscommunication, lengthy delays, and in many cases, nonaction.

MINUTES

The board secretary is typically responsible for taking the minutes. For some reason boards often have the property manager or their assistant take the meeting minutes, but in my opinion, it is a better practice to keep that responsibility within the board. If the secretary is not available, have another board volunteer to take the minutes.

These days, there are great productivity tools like Otter.ai that automatically transcribe notes from online meetings in Zoom, Google Meet, or Microsoft Teams. Using a tool like this not only helps with the minutes but also helps eliminate the small talk between the agenda items, which can lead to shorter and more efficient board meetings. (Who wants to waste time reading in the minutes about a neighbor leaving a pair of shoes in the hallway for days, when it's already been taken care of?)

TIME

We recommend keeping meetings to an hour or less, as few people can stay productive for longer than that. (It is not uncommon for a disorganized and divided board to have monthly meetings that take over two hours and for them to table half the agenda items. Don't be that board.) Our top tips to keep the meeting under an hour include:

- Stick to the agenda.
- Organize the agenda with the mandatory tasks first; for instance, any board decisions that were voted on via email since the last board meeting need to be recorded in the minutes first, followed by the urgent and essential tasks, with everything else being last on the agenda.
- On the agenda, state the time allotted (e.g., one to five minutes) to the right of each agenda item.
- Assign one person to use a timer app with the sound on, and enforce the limit when the timer sounds.
- Table any nonurgent agenda items that require more research, which should be done outside of the monthly meeting.

Consider this: a sharp business owner makes decisions frequently and quickly. Decisiveness is an effective strategy for moving their business forward; procrastination is not. Endless discussion over minor details is inefficient and not something a productive, well-run organization would tolerate—so don't. To quote one of the great doers in our nation's history, Theodore Roosevelt, "In any moment of decision, the best thing you can do is the right thing, the next best thing is the wrong thing, and the worst thing you can do is nothing."

THE ANNUAL GENERAL MEETING

The primary purpose of the annual general meeting (AGM) is to elect the co-op or condo's board for the upcoming year.

AGM AGENDA

The AGM starts with declaring a quorum so that the meeting counts as an AGM. For the AGM you must reach a quorum of owners (not just board members); your bylaws will specify the number, but it is likely to be 50 percent, 67 percent, or 75 percent of owners. If a quorum is not reached, the meeting becomes an informational meeting and the existing board continues until the next AGM.

The second item on the AGM agenda is to approve the minutes from the last AGM. The board then typically reports on some of the repair projects or upgrades that they have been working on or have planned. The auditor may report on the financial status of the association, and the attorney may report on any legal issues. Then, there's the vote for board members. Finally, the floor is opened for Q&A from owners.

AGM INVITATION

In New York, the invitation for the AGM must be sent to all owners or members between ten and sixty days prior to the meeting date. We recommend sending the invitation one month before the meeting to facilitate a nomination deadline two to three weeks before the meeting. Any shorter notification period implies that the board doesn't care, is disorganized, or is not managing the building proactively. This does not signal a successful board that truly wants to serve its constituents.

Best board practice is to send out the AGM invitation with instructions on how to nominate volunteers, whether yourself or your neighbor, to the board. Set a deadline, for instance, ten days before the election, and a minimum requirement for submitting the nomination, such as a bio, qualifications, and a statement why they are running and why others should vote for them. Once you have set a deadline for nominations, be sure all communications clearly state that nominations will not be accepted after the deadline or at the annual meeting.

An often-overlooked nomination requirement might seem obvious as soon as you read this: All those who nominate themselves (or are nominated) must be current in paying their monthly dues. Anyone in arrears will be disqualified. This practice serves one of two purposes: it eliminates a troublesome board nominee, or it solves an arrearage problem. Either way, it will save the rest of the board time and money.

PREPARING FOR THE MEETING

Your annual meeting is in a few days. If you are on the board and feeling a bit stressed as the day approaches, you're probably not alone. You might be worried about how the meeting will go and what kind of questions you'll get; you may even be losing sleep.

If you are a co-op or condo owner, you might be preparing a list of tough questions that you've been scribbling down since last year's meeting adjourned before the board addressed all your concerns. A full year of accumulated frustration can easily turn into anger. You might even be commiserating with some of your neighbors about your problems with the board.

One board president, Jo Ann, called to tell me that she was dreading the building's upcoming meetings. Although every board operates differently, this board always scheduled two meetings:

an informational meeting where owners were informed of the forthcoming projects for the building and, two weeks later, the annual meeting dedicated to voting on those projects. Past experience with arguments, offensive language, and finger-pointing at the board from owners had brought Jo Ann many sleepless nights.

Some advice...

KNOW WHAT QUESTIONS TO EXPECT

As trusted advisors to boards, we listen to our clients. They tell us stories, share the types of questions they get, and let us know how anxious they are about the dreaded annual meeting.

It turns out that the most common questions for the board in one building are heard in most other buildings as well:

- When will the scaffolding be removed?
- Why did you refinance the underlying mortgage?
- Why can't we have your email addresses and phone numbers?
- Why is the boiler set so my apartment never gets warm enough?
- Why is it so hot in my apartment that I must crack my windows open in the winter?
- Why can't we get energy-efficient windows?
- Why are our monthly dues increasing again?
- Why don't you write a newsletter? (Here's a response that every board should use: "That's a great idea! Can we count on you to head up writing this newsletter?")

I heard this question only once, but I found it funny, so I thought I'd share it: Since you are replacing the elevators, can you make them bigger? (For elevator novices, the size of the elevator shaft dictates the size of the elevator, so unless every apartment next to the elevator is willing to give up a portion of their space, the answer to this question would be a definite NO.)

Additionally, be sure to identify any timely building-specific issues you know will arise. By preparing answers in advance, you'll feel more confident and will be able to answer residents' questions more efficiently and effectively.

PREPARE A PRESENTATION

One high-impact approach I recommend is to prepare a few presentation slides for the annual meeting. You wouldn't conduct an informational business meeting without slides, yet we often see co-op and condo boards show up without slides that might help them communicate during their annual meeting. Slides demonstrate to owners that you are prepared, organized, and care enough about your community to have put some time and effort into planning the meeting.

For Jo Ann's informational meeting, we put together a simple five-slide presentation. The first slide set the expectations and tone for the meeting with the agenda and time frames for each of the three vendors being considered. To alleviate the burden from the board, I ran the meeting, managed the slide sharing, and made sure the agenda items were covered in the time allotted. I also coordinated the questions for each vendor on the schedule and brought them into the Zoom meeting at their designated time. Everything went so well that we finished on time, with all questions answered, and it was deemed the most successful meeting in the building's history.

BRING IN EXPERTS

Another way to relieve the pressure on the board at the annual meeting is to bring in third-party professionals to speak directly to attendees about their area of expertise. It is customary to have the auditor and legal counsel at the annual meeting, but why not bring in other professionals when appropriate? If your building is undergoing or planning structural, façade, or leak repairs, bringing in the exterior engineer to answer some questions for five or ten minutes could be very helpful. If your building is planning energy conservation measures, or cosmetic upgrades to the lobby and hallways, inviting those professionals to the meeting for some Q&A also takes the pressure off the board. Note: If you are meeting via video, it is not an imposition for these professsionals to pop in for a few minutes—it's much less effort than showing up at an in-person meeting.

COMMUNICATE YEAR-ROUND

When an AGM becomes confrontational between owners and the board, the problem often comes down to communication and listening, or lack thereof. When owners are limited to bringing their questions and concerns to the board once a year, their problems often percolate and become more urgent than they ever needed to be. Between meetings there might be chatter between owners in the hallways and laundry rooms, and the old game of telephone often exacerbates problems. In most cases, this situation can be solved by improved, regular communication between the board and owners. In our experience, the more the board communicates and involves the community, the more productive and cordial the community becomes. The annual meetings also tend to become shorter. We recently attended an annual meeting that was over in just forty-two minutes! We'll cover some specific ways to communicate with residents in the next section as well as in Chapter 8.

BOARD COMMUNICATION

Being on the board and representing your community entails a particular responsibility for communication. An ideal board member is one who is a great listener, asks questions, manages their emotions, listens for ideas and opportunities, and remains open to the conversation. Not everyone on the board needs excellent communication skills, but the more the better, and at least one member should be practiced.

A great communicator considers who they are talking to and what that person's body language may be signaling to them. They are brief and specific. They take notes and think before they speak. They also know when it's better not to reply by email but instead to pick up the phone or meet in person. (This is the reason that when we staged our "coup," my husband and I decided that he would serve on the board, not me. I have since worked on my communication skills and believe I have become better at thinking before speaking.)

One way to keep the conversation positive and productive is to replace the word "but" with "yes, and . . . ." For example, when someone's complaint is "We have no way of contacting the board," instead of replying with "But we don't want everyone to have access to our email addresses," try this instead: "Yes, and that's why we have a 'Contact Management' button on the building's online portal—so you can always reach the board members, even when they change."

A great email or text communicator checks their response twice and asks another board member to read and approve it before hitting send. I am not sure if you can relate, but early in my career, I sent off an email that turned into a long back-and-forth email thread that got only more heated and aggressive with each response. It required more time to undo the damage than if I had just called an in-person meeting. As you have no doubt discovered yourself, emails can sound much harsher than the writer intends, so asking for another set of eyes on your communication can help you maintain a professional tone.

Regardless of whether you are speaking in person or communicating in written form, your job as a board member is to serve the residents, so always reply to questions and complaints, as a problem that seems minor to you may be significant to someone else. We have seen many boards that are not responsive to owners' concerns, and the consequences are often much more significant than the problem itself would have been. One shareholder complained when the city moved the building's garbage collection to just outside his window. The board had nothing to do with this change, so they intentionally decided to ignore the complaint. They never got back to the owner, who got angry and sued the building! No one wants to end up in an unnecessary lawsuit. A simple explanation would have avoided this problem.

One method of exploring and resolving complaints and problems is to respond with a question: How would you handle this? What do you suggest that we do in this situation? Are you saying you would like to volunteer to take care of this?

Finally, residents will appreciate proactive communications from the board. Some of the best ways for the board to share information are also methods for engaging the entire community. We talk more about community engagement ideas in Chapter 8.

PRODUCTIVITY TOOLS AND TECHNOLOGY

If you own your own company, you understand the value of tools and systems that help your business operate efficiently. If you are employed by a company, you are using similar tools and systems that your employer has put in place. In either case, your reliance on these tools is likely driven by key performance indicators.

KEY PERFORMANCE INDICATORS

Put simply, a *key performance indicator (KPI)* provides a metric to objectively gauge whether your tools, projects, systems, and even your employees are providing the value you expect from them. To ensure your co-op or condo board is operating effectively and efficiently, consider establishing KPIs and tracking them over time in a spreadsheet. For example:

- **Budget:** Check monthly if you meet your budget. Score yourself a 1 for all months where the budget is within 2% of the budget; score yourself a 0 if you are over or under budget by more than 2%.
- **Number of meetings:** Track the number of meetings you have. The board should have at least one meeting per month, but if you have important projects going on,

you might want to hold weekly or bi-monthly meetings during those times. Meetings help you move the needle forward, so if you see a string of zeros, you know you have a problem.

- **Number of votes on important issues:** Track the number of important decisions you make each month. Successful businesses make decisions quickly and frequently, so if you make decisions only once per month it may take a long time to make a positive impact for your building and community.
- **Dues payment:** Track the number of residents who do not pay their monthly dues, or do not pay them in a timely manner. Troublesome patterns may spur you to improving your collection practices. My firm worked with one building that had twelve troublesome late payers when we started; now they're down to one.
- **Apartment sales:** Track the average sales price per square foot in the building. Keeping track of every sale will help you gauge sales prices over time. You might even get the historical sales prices from the property manager, and the square footage is listed in the offering documents. Keeping a spreadsheet of this data over time might seem like extra work, but in the end, knowing the average sales price per square foot is an important part of knowing the results of your board's efforts.

As you may have heard before, "What doesn't get measured doesn't get done." Regular measurement and reporting keeps you focused on your organization's goals and helps you make informed decisions. It also helps you detect when it is time to make adjustments for a better outcome. So let's look at some tools that can help you run your building efficiently and effectively and achieve the targets you set for your KPIs.

BENCHMARKING

When our "coup" group took over our board and started looking at the expenses, we decided to create a benchmark, a collection of data about other buildings against which we could compare our building. Benchmarking was a concept I had learned from my experience as a business analyst on Wall Street. How else would we know if the cost of a particular service, let's say $10,000, was high, low, or average? You may be able to gather this information on a smaller scale for yourself. If you don't have the time to do that, this may be an opportunity to bring in a consultant (like The Folson Group!) who has this data collected already.

CLOUD STORAGE

Cloud storage is crucial to operating an effective community. With access to the cloud, by organizing folders in a sensible way and assigning documents appropriate and logical names, we're able to access what we need from any location and easily share and collaborate with our teams. In today's world, where most companies operate in the cloud, I'm reminded of how frustrating it was before. How did we even do business?

PROJECT MANAGEMENT TOOLS

Cloud-based project management tools are key to productivity and success on any project, big or small. While there are many different project management tools available, they all share the basic features of providing a clear, concise way to manage deadlines, tasks, and team communication. They also help keep everyone on the same page, reducing the chances of misunderstandings and errors. In a nutshell, project management tools can save valuable time and resources.

Some of the most popular project management tools include Trello, Asana, and Basecamp. These platforms offer a variety of features and integrations to suit the needs of any team. In addition to productivity benefits, project management tools can also help with budgeting and tracking progress over time. The ability to access detailed records of the tasks and costs associated with a project helps managers identify areas where money is being wasted or deadlines are not being met. Used correctly, project management tools can be a powerful asset for any business or individual.

COLLABORATIVE TOOLS

Collaborative tools enable teams to work with other team members online. For instance, Google Workspace and Microsoft 365 allow for multiple people to review and edit the same file simultaneously. Other collaborative tools include QuickBooks, Canva, and pretty much any other tool that users connect to via the cloud.

VIDEO CONFERENCING

Communication is an important part of teams being able to collaborate, and video conferencing can be more efficient than in-person meetings, especially for quick conversations or working together online (but don't neglect the need for in-person meetings when appropriate). In 2020, at the onset of the pandemic, Zoom came out of nowhere and took work-from-home culture to a whole new level. In response, Google and Microsoft improved their video conferencing tools as well.

SCHEDULING TOOLS

Scheduling tools make it easy for someone to get on your calendar without multiple rounds of emails suggesting dates and times. Before the pandemic, I'd seen some people using these tools, but I hadn't made the leap myself. When the pandemic hit and we were ordered to stay at home, I realized that instead of having four in-person meetings per day, I could have eight virtual meetings. I investigated tools and decided to try out Calendly for scheduling. I love it! It saves me a lot of time and allows the boards I consult with to easily find times that work for their team. There are plenty of other tools to consider: Acuity Scheduling, Appointy, and more. Pro tip: Many of these tools also integrate with Zoom and other tools.

LISTS AND SPREADSHEETS

I don't know about you, but I love lists. They are the simple tool I can't live without. They help me not only to stay organized, and to strategize and prioritize, but they also help me get things done. My lists used to be extremely long, but after reading David Allen's book *Getting Things Done: The Art of Stress-Free Productivity*, I now keep my list to three main items. Anything beyond that is a bonus. Each night, I reflect on my day's accomplishments, after which I write a new list of the three most important things I want to accomplish the next day.

I also keep lists or indexes in a few different spreadsheets. My firm keeps a project management sheet for every building. In it we have the financial statements, a list of service contracts and vendors, and any deadlines or expiration dates. These are integrated with our Google calendars so that we don't miss any deadlines, as some can be a year out. Our daily task list always includes the buildings we will concentrate on the next day.

In my opinion, the most important list a building must keep is one with an inventory of the building's systems. It is possible that the property manager has some of the information, which they can share with you. The super or resident manager likely keeps a separate list. To me, having multiple lists only creates more work and increases the likelihood of conflicting information between lists. My suggestion is to consolidate any duplicate lists into one master list with cloud-based storage and file-sharing capabilities so the appropriate people can access it as needed. If you (the board) set this up and act as the administrator, you can assign permissions to various parties, such as the super, property manager, or various board members, allowing them to view or edit certain items as you deem appropriate. If this is set up as a Google Sheets file, due dates can be integrated with your Google calendar. This system can be particularly helpful, as some compliance due dates may require as much as three, six, or even twelve months of lead time.

Let's look at an elevator, for example. When it comes to an elevator, the most important information to track is the installation date, expected life, and due dates for Cat-1 and Cat-5 testing (the required annual and five-year inspections, respectively). A separate column showing the deadlines for any upcoming new regulations may also be in order. Elevators also have many subsystems with a shorter lifespan than the actual elevator, including cables, motors, and all the other items that are listed on the elevator service agreement; these should be tracked too. For instance, if one of the motors was replaced a couple of years ago, tracking that replacement, the date it occurred, and the cost is useful for estimating anticipated costs for motor replacements in your building's other elevators. Nobody likes surprises.

In 2019, we requested the elevator service agreement from a client, who had assigned one board member, Anthony, to be our liaison so as to not overwhelm the entire board with emails. Anthony seemed surprised by this request, as he was not even aware that such an agreement existed. When he sent us the agreement, we saw that it was dated 1999!

There's an agreement for everything. Even something that might seem quite minor, like pest extermination services, comes with an agreement. If it happens that neither the property manager nor the vendor has a copy of the agreement, it could be the result of their transitioning from filing cabinets to online document storage. In that case, the vendor will typically provide a new agreement to be signed. No vendor wants to work without an agreement that spells out the terms and fees.

If your board has a long list of building upgrades that need to be addressed, create a list in a Google sheet and assign each item to a board member to research. Assign someone only an upgrade item they truly care about, or it won't get done. I have included a template list of common building systems and their estimated useful life in the free workbook that accompanies this book.

PLANNING TOOLS

Co-op and condo boards often become overwhelmed because their organizations are so complex; focusing and staying on track can be challenging when there are so many distractions. In addition to suggesting you make lists (my favorite!), I want to introduce two planning tools that can help keep you focused: the Eisenhower Box and SMART goals. Both of these are used regularly in business settings, so you may be familiar with them from your work environment.

EISENHOWER BOX

You've got a huge list of projects to tackle—inspections, maintenance, capital investments. How do you decide what is first? Use the same approach the very efficient and productive President Eisenhower did.

Start by placing each item on your list into one of the following categories:
- Important and Urgent
- Important but Not Urgent
- Not Important but Urgent
- Not Important and Not Urgent

Your top priorities are in the first category and the priority level decreases as you move down the list. Key point: focus on what's *important*!

To get a visual representation, place your action list into a 2x2 matrix. This is commonly referred to as the Eisenhower Box, or the Eisenhower Matrix. Figure 1 presents an Eisenhower Box with some of the common issues that co-ops and condos encounter.

**Figure 1: Sample Eisenhower Box for Co-ops and Condos
(Source: The Folson Group)**

	Urgent	Not Urgent
Important	Fires Leaks Bed Bugs Staff Accidents LAWS FISP LL11 BACKFLOW 1	Capital Projects Roofs, elevators, windows, heating Oil-gas Budgeting Bylaws Proprietary Lease 2
Not Important	Resident & Staff 3 Complaints Lawsuits Staff turnover	4 Updating website House Rules CHANGING SERVICE PROVIDERS

You'll notice that the top left quadrant, Important and Urgent, includes things like fires, leaks, bed bugs, and following the law with inspections and such.

The top right quadrant, Important but Not Urgent, includes things like capital projects, budgeting, and reviewing bylaws—those things you know need to be done but don't necessarily have a burning platform.

The bottom left quadrant, Not Important but Urgent, includes dealing with complaints, lawsuits, and staff turnover.

Finally, the bottom right quadrant, Not Important and Not Urgent, includes things like updating the website and changing service providers.

The board of one of our buildings was working on revising their bylaws when the boiler broke down. For obvious reasons, as the boiler heats the building and provides hot water, a boiler repair is more urgent than updated bylaws. But please don't misunderstand—just because something in is the Not Important boxes doesn't mean it *never* needs to be done; the quadrants simply help you prioritize.

And there is no reason a complex organization like a residential multi-family building can't tackle multiple projects simultaneously. We currently have a client who is revising bylaws, planning a hallway and lobby renovation, installing Building-Link (an online platform for residential administration), and working on settling a lawsuit. At the same time, we are working with them on upgrading their electricity and offering a better insurance proposal.

SMART GOALS

It becomes easier to achieve success when you've defined—and everyone agrees to—exactly what you are trying to accomplish. Using SMART goals is one way to get everyone on board.

SMART is an acronym for:
- **Specific:** Focused on a particular area
- **Measurable:** A quantifiable way to demonstrate achievement
- **Achievable:** Within your control and realistic in nature
- **Results-focused:** Focused on achieving an outcome
- **Time-bound:** Having a clear deadline or time frame

(You may occasionally see variations with Assignable, Reasonable, Realistic, or Relevant, or Time-related, but you get the idea.)

A so-so goal might be "Be more energy efficient." That's nice but doesn't help you focus your resources or attention.

A SMART version might be "Reduce energy usage by 20% by replacing all common area light bulbs with LED bulbs by December 1." The goal is specific to the area of focus; an improvement target was set; changing light bulbs is eminently doable; the action is focused toward getting results of reducing usage (from the original vague goal); and a deadline was set for completing the effort and measuring results.

Other SMART goals could be:
- Reduce water usage by 10% by installing low-flow toilets in 50% of apartments over the next year.
- Enhance community cohesion by holding two social events next year with resident attendance of 60%+.
- Fund a hallway renovation without increasing monthly fees by identifying $10,000 in annual cost savings in budget expense line items by end of Q2. (That $10,000 might not sound like a lot, but once you find that first $10,000, you'll feel successful and go for the next $10,000. Plus, the effect of compounding is magical.)

By combining your prioritized actions from the Eisenhower Box with SMART goals, you will be unstoppable!

Incorporating all the tools and strategies that serve you so well in your professional life into your volunteer role as a co-op or condo board member will eliminate a lot of uncertainty and stress. And if you are an owner who is not yet serving on the board, asking the board about the tools and tech they use is a good way to gauge how well they are running your building. Remember, it's likely your largest lifetime investment.

■ ■ ■

WORKBOOK RESOURCES

Our free downloadable workbook contains:
- Sample Meeting Agenda
- Sample Meeting Minutes
- Sample Code of Conduct
- Sample Code of Ethics
- Sample Building Systems and Their Estimated Useful Life
- And more!

To download the workbook, use the QR code below or visit https://www.thefolsongroup.com/book.

PART THREE

THE BOARD'S MAJOR AREAS OF RESPONSIBILITY

*"If you're proactive, you focus on preparing.
If you're reactive, you end up focusing on repairing."*

—John C. Maxwell

IN PART THREE, WE LOOK AT the major areas of responsibility for any co-op or condo board: safety, finance, quality of life, and sustainability.

■ ■ ■

CHAPTER 6

SAFETY FIRST

"One of the tests of leadership is the ability to recognize a problem before it becomes an emergency."

—Arnold H. Glasow

IMAGINE YOU VOLUNTEERED to join your association's board simply to serve on the decorating committee. When you submitted your nomination, you probably thought your focus would be replacing that old couch in the lobby or the 1980s-era wallpaper in the residential hallways, or spearheading weeding the garden or selecting flower arrangements.

And then a report deeming your building unsafe puts a spoke in that wheel.

In addition to the cost associated with a building repair, planning for the construction will require many hours, over many months; that's additional time away from your own job, obligations, family, and hobbies (and the decorating committee). You could probably deal with a big project if you knew that it would take four or even twelve months to plan; however, in the early stages, the timeline for a big repair project is hard to estimate accurately. Who knows how many hours, months, or even years it will take? With rare exceptions, the board does not have adequate qualifications to plan and oversee a project of this significance without outside assistance.

As a board member, how will you deal with this information?

YOUR FIRST DUTY

A co-op or condo board's first duty is safety. Recall, board members are fiduciaries and must act in the owners' and members' best interest. It's in no one's best interest to live in an unsafe building.

The board's initial response to a safety report may be to ask whether the engineer's analysis of the unsafe structure is accurate. This is a legitimate question. When you receive a troubling diagnosis from your doctor, do you just accept it, or do you seek a second opinion from a different doctor? Several of my friends and family members who sought a second opinion have found that they did not need the surgery or medication the first doctor recommended. The same goes for an engineering report deeming a building unsafe.

The difference, of course, is that if you need surgery, you can decide to delay your own treatment as a personal choice, with no effect on others. A co-op or condo board that chooses to delay an urgent repair recommended by their engineer is risking the safety of their neighbors and the soundness of the entire building. In the case of the Champlain Towers South collapse, we see how delay can result in the worst outcome imaginable.

In New York City, we've also had some terrible accidents.
- On May 16, 1979, a freshman from Barnard College was fatally struck by a piece of terra-cotta that fell from the eighth story of a building on West 115th Street.

- On December 14, 2011, a woman in Midtown was crushed between the elevator and the shaft when the elevator unexpectedly rose as she stepped into it.
- On March 12, 2014, an explosion in the East Harlem neighborhood leveled two apartment buildings, killing eight people, injuring at least seventy others, and displacing a hundred families.

While there is no going back, it's worth noting that in each of these cases, subsequent investigation into the incidents led to various safety reforms being enacted in New York City, with most of them falling under the New York City Department of Buildings' (DOB) jurisdiction.

Compliance and license filings with the NYC DOB fall under three categories: Build, Safety, and Licensing, with Safety comprising the following:

- Boiler
- Elevator
- Energy – Building Emissions
- Façades

All filings entered in the safety database are publicly available on the DOB website.[6] Anyone can access the records for any building and see the violations related to those four categories.

Co-op and condo owners, especially those serving as board members, should familiarize themselves with the following safety requirements and programs. The first two I'll describe (façade and elevator) are included in the NYC DOB safety database noted above; the other three (gas, fire safety, and construction) are not.

---

[6] https://a810-dobnow.nyc.gov/publish/Index.html#!/

FAÇADE INSPECTION SAFETY PROGRAM

In accordance with the NYC DOB Façade Inspection Safety Program (FISP), formerly Local Law 11 of 1998, within the five boroughs of New York City, every five years a façade inspection must be performed on all buildings that are greater than six stories in height and on any individual wall(s) greater than six stories in height on otherwise exempt buildings. These inspections must be accompanied by a report submitted to the Department of Buildings describing the building as either safe, safe with a repair and maintenance program (SWARMP), or unsafe. All conditions observed must also be individually identified with the applicable classification. The report must include a description of required repair work, along with a timeline for performing the repairs, and it must be signed by the building owner and the professional engineer or registered architect responsible for the inspection.

I contacted our friends at Sullivan Engineering, a Rimkus Company, about FISP. Brian Sullivan, a commonsense, practical problem-solver, provided me with the description above and offered some valuable tips on how to best keep a building's exterior safe and the repairs to a minimum.

- Begin all projects with the end in mind. Think about what your objective is for the project.
- It is better to be proactive than reactive, so periodic reviews are always recommended.
- Proper planning allows for economies of scale and the elimination of unnecessary extra costs. For example, with a long-term plan, it is possible to work on two projects concurrently or consecutively, thereby requiring

- Just because your building does not exceed six stories in height, that does not mean you can ignore safety concerns related to its exterior. If you have cracking terra-cotta, it needs to be addressed. If your façade hasn't been inspected or repaired in ten or twenty years, it's time for a professional inspection.
- If you have leaks, hope is not a good strategy, and neither are quick fixes. There is no time like the present to take care of problems once and for all.

While we've discussed New York City's specific program, many other cities and states have façade ordinances, so be sure to become familiar with yours.

ELEVATORS

In response to an increase in elevator accidents, due in part to aging elevators, the DOB added four regulations in recent years.

- In 2009, the DOB adopted the Category 1 and Category 5 inspections, commonly known as Cat-1 and Cat-5 periodic inspections. Cat-1 is an annual inspection, and Cat-5 is a more in-depth inspection performed every five years.
- January 1, 2020, marked the deadline to install a door lock monitor (DLM).
- As of January 1, 2022, the periodic inspections must be performed by an approved elevator agency that is *not* affiliated with the agency performing the elevator maintenance.

- And effective January 1, 2027, all traction elevators are required to have an emergency brake.

These regulations and inspections might seem like a hassle, but they are all there to keep every one of us safe. Part of the board's job is to keep up with new regulations, so make sure that these are all on your list.

PERIODIC GAS INSPECTION

Local Law 152 (LL152) was passed in 2016 in response to an increase in fatal gas explosions. The law requires that New York City buildings with more than two dwelling units have their gas piping system periodically inspected by an NYC-licensed master plumber (LMP), with the initial inspection occurring during one of the subsequent four years, and periodically every four years following, with initial submission dates determined by Community District Location. The first round of inspections was in 2020.

Bill Weidner, a friend of The Folson Group, co-founded KeepMyGas.nyc in response to the law. The firm is a master plumbing company specializing in LL152. Here are Bill's recommendations for navigating the new requirements and engaging an LMP for this inspection:

- Look up when your periodic inspection is due.
- Check the LMP's credentials; get the license and verify it in the DOB licensee portal.
- Verify that the LMP will use a Public Service Commission–approved portable combustible gas detection device during the inspection.
- Verify that the LMP will file the required reports and provide you with a copy of the filing.

- Request the plumber's certificate of insurance (COI) for both general liability (GL) *and* professional liability, as inspections are not covered by the LMP's GL insurance.

Local Law 152 is in full effect with inspections taking place during the last sixty days of the year. If this is your year, make sure to ask your property manager and super to schedule this inspection, as we all want to keep our residents safe and as far away from gas leaks as possible.

FIRE SAFETY

When it comes to fire safety, the local fire department is generally the entity that implements and enforces regulations. In New York City, it is the New York City Fire Department that enforces the fire codes and educates the public on safety measures.

The areas addressed by fire codes and safety measures are wide-ranging and include the following:
- Fire extinguishers
- Smoke and carbon monoxide alarms
- Sprinklers
- Alarms
- Cooking gas
- Natural gas
- Emergency exit signs

Another category that falls under the fire department's jurisdiction is hallway clearance and signage. For instance, you are not allowed to store any items in the hallways, including shoes, umbrellas, or strollers. On a recent building tour, the super took us to one floor where a permanent shoe rack had been installed in the hallway by one of the doors. When we informed the super that the building could get fined for that because it violated the fire code, he shrugged his shoulders and said that there was nothing he could do about it because it belonged to the board president. Holy smokes! (Pun entirely intended.)

New York City's multifamily buildings are required to display directional marking and signs as outlined in Section FC 505 of the code. Signs must be placed at a specific height just above the floor marking each apartment and common area door. This measure is intended to assist emergency response personnel in locating apartments when responding to fires, medical emergencies, and other emergencies.

Fire safety is extremely important. Be sure your building has an inventory of all the relevant systems with dates of installation and end of expected life, so that you can plan for systems to be replaced without interruption.

CONSTRUCTION CODES

As you can imagine, safety is the top priority when it comes to construction. The New York City Construction Codes address construction standards and regulations to keep the city and its residents safe. As of this writing, the latest code is the 2022 Construction Code, which covers the New York City General Administrative Provisions, Plumbing, Building, Mechanical, and Fuel Gas Codes.

Additional codes exist beyond this cursory list, and each professional knows which code they are required to adhere to. For example, the electrical code is separate from the safety and construction codes. A qualified electrician understands this and knows how to navigate any repairs or projects in compliance with the code. That's why it is so important to work with qualified, licensed professionals on all of your building's projects.

THE PROFESSIONALS WHO MAKE IT HAPPEN

As you know by now, as fiduciaries, the board is responsible for the safety of the building: structure, façades, roofs, elevators, plumbing, and HVAC and boiler systems. Obviously, the board is not expected to do this work themselves, so they surround themselves with a long list of professionals and vendors that specialize in particular areas.

The property manager is responsible for making sure that the building adheres to all safety codes and gets all required inspections. For example, they typically initiate and schedule the FISP inspection and keep the board apprised of the inspection details as the date approaches. As recently as a decade ago, property management firms managed the building code compliance in-house, but these days, the PM can create an account with a third-party service for each of their buildings that notifies them of compliance deadlines as well as any violations for noncompliance. The super may also be involved in routine inspections or coordinating service providers. And as described earlier, the PM is often involved in coordinating larger projects.

For inspections, you need to hire the appropriately qualified and licensed professionals, according to the relevant code. For repairs or major safety upgrades, you may need to hire architects, structural engineers, mechanical engineers, exterior engineers, elevator consultants or mechanics, and more. By engaging all the appropriate specialists to identify and address potential hazards, and by ensuring preventive maintenance and repairs are done in a timely manner, a board can be confident they are providing the safest conditions for themselves and their neighbors.

Most old buildings have old systems, many of which have been neglected for years and need to be replaced. The problem facing most boards is that there are often not enough reserve funds to cover the cost of upgrades. In addition, the board often doesn't have the time, will, or commitment to take on projects they see as not urgent or required by law.

It's important to plan ahead. If the elevator has a projected twenty-five-year life span and it's been in service sixty years, plan to replace it instead of resorting to Band-Aid repairs. If it's only twenty-five years old, don't coast through year twenty-six and just wait for it to malfunction. Research options for replacing it, including how the work will be funded. You may not need to replace it at the twenty-five-year mark, but having the ability to do so if required constitutes good planning.

Since safety and finances are often the two factors we are always balancing, let's look at finances next.

■ ■ ■

WORKBOOK RESOURCES

Our free downloadable workbook contains:
- Sample Building Systems and Their Estimated Useful Life
- Checklist for Switching Vendors
- And more!

To download the workbook, use the QR code below or visit https://www.thefolsongroup.com/book.

CHAPTER 7

FINANCES

"The time to repair the roof is when the sun is shining."

—John F. Kennedy

PRIOR TO CO-FOUNDING The Folson Group, any time I was out networking, I would introduce myself as the financial advisor that I was. You can imagine how thrilled people were to be meeting yet another financial advisor, so to avoid the predictable eye roll, I started introducing myself with some version of "Hi, nice to meet you. I helped my co-op board save $340,000!" Nearly every response I received was "Can I introduce you to *my* co-op board?" That's when I got the idea to start The Folson Group. In the years since, our team has helped many co-op and condo associations save money while maintaining safety and improving the quality of life in their building.

In this chapter we'll review the basics of financial management in a co-op or condo association, look at ways to fund capital projects, and share ideas for saving money so that you have more funds available to use to get projects done while keeping owner expenses down.

THE PROFESSIONALS WHO MAKE IT HAPPEN

As you already know, the board of directors has a fiduciary responsibility to look out for the well-being of the co-op or condo association, and they are responsible for making sure the books are kept and the taxes are paid. But they are unlikely to do all this work themselves.

As described earlier in this book, most likely the property management team or a bookkeeper will keep the books. A CPA will be engaged for tax filings and audits. And an attorney may be involved for various contractual purposes.

BANK ACCOUNTS

As with any business, a co-op or condo association needs a bank. Likely your banking relationship will already be established when you join the board, but here are a few things to know and to keep in mind in case you are considering a new one.

TYPES OF ACCOUNTS

When new board members first see the association's monthly financial reports, they are often puzzled why the association has so many bank accounts.

Returning to one of the themes of this book, your building is a business. Even a small business typically has at least one checking account, perhaps a savings account, and a business loan or line of credit as well as credit cards. Co-op and condo buildings don't typically have credit cards, but they do have multiple checking or savings accounts. These accounts serve multiple purposes and can be divided into these categories:

Operating account. The operating account is used for—as you might expect—everyday operations—the money coming in and going out on a daily basis. The operating account could be one account, or it could be multiple accounts. For instance, in a co-op there could be separate accounts for the real estate tax payments and the mortgage payments.

Reserve account. A reserve account is typically designated for a special purpose, and, again, there could one account or multiple. For example, some co-ops and condos have a separate reserve account specifically for assessments that are dictated by the bylaws.

Escrow account. Escrow accounts are accounts in which funds are held until certain conditions are met. With co-op and condo associations, escrow accounts tend to be opened for individual owners for special purposes. For example, when a buyer does not meet specific rules, such as an income ratio, the board may ask for some amount to be put into an escrow account until the rule has been met.

Another reason to have multiple accounts is that bank accounts are FDIC-insured for up to $250,000 at each bank. A quarter of a million might sound like a lot, but in running a building, the account balances can run quite high. Spreading the funds around minimizes the risk should something go wrong at the bank.

BANK FEES

In selecting a bank, assess the services you need and the fees charged. Bank fees can be high or low depending on the bank and the account balance. Since most co-op and condo accounts have a large daily average balance, they avoid ongoing account maintenance fees. However, be sure to keep an eye out. One of our clients was paying $2,500 per year in bank fees. The bank's daily minimum to avoid fees was only $2,000, and this association had a balance of more than $100,000! All it took was a phone call to the banker to get the account coded correctly to avoid the fees.

PAYMENT METHODS

There are a variety of ways to make payments and receive money, some of which have fees attached. You may use paper checks or debit cards, but consider whether you need other options for moving funds electronically as well.

Wires. Wire transfers are often used to send large amounts of money quickly and securely from one bank account to another. Bank wire fees have two fees to them: one for the sending bank and one for the receiving bank. For our bank, wiring money out is $5, but if someone wires money to our company, the incoming wire fee is $25 (meaning the receiving party gets $25 less than expected). We used to see more wires in the past, but they seem to be giving way to other payment forms.

ACHs. Automated clearing house (ACH) transfers move money electronically between bank accounts or other financial institutions. They have been around for over fifty years, but in the digital world we live in, they seem to have become more common. For instance, you may use ACHs if your employer direct deposits your paycheck. ACHs typically take a couple of days, so a bit longer than a wire transfer, but they are usually free of charge to the sender and receiver if they are to and from a bank. The reason they are "free" is that the bank collects the overnight interest rate on the money; this is called the "float." When the ACH is to or from a fund-processing firm, the payment processor charges a fee. (Many, if not most, NYC property management firms use payment processing services for their client buildings.)

Other payment tools. There are a variety of direct payment tools, such as Venmo, Zelle, and PayPal, that you may use personally, and some of them are becoming more common in business. Zelle transfers are instantaneous, and Zelle does not charge fees (though individual banks providing the Zelle may, so be sure to check before using it), but it is currently available only through a handful of the largest banks in the country and both sender and receiver must have accounts in that bank network.

At The Folson Group on our invoices, we list Zelle and Venmo as options to pay us, but we have yet to receive one payment from a property management firm using anything but old-fashioned checks in the mail. From our self-managed co-op and condo clients, we receive Zelle, Venmo, and QuickBooks payments regularly.

ACCOUNTS RECEIVABLE AND ACCOUNTS PAYABLE

The board of directors is responsible for collection of all owners' fees and payment of all expenses for their association, but these responsibilities are often delegated to the property manager.

As owners' dues are critical to the functioning of the building, it's important owners stay up to date on their payments. If an owner is in arrears, the PM normally has a standard procedure with template letters that they send. If those in arrears do not pay up, the matter is typically referred to an attorney. Ultimately, though, collection of owners' dues is still the responsibility of the board.

Property management firms sometimes have accounts receivable (AR) and accounts payable (AP) departments to handle those functions, but in many cases, they outsource the AR and AP administration to a third-party vendor. The idea of a third-party processor is that you pay a small fee on each transaction in order to get faster processing. But one of the most common problems that we hear from boards is that ever since their property management firm switched to an AP processor service they can't get their vendors paid. In New York City, there is one firm that is at the forefront of AP automation servicing, and in my opinion, it is a brilliant service. I believe most payment problems stem from the fact that the property management firms have not set up the roles, responsibilities, and authorization processes needed to adequately service their clients.

For example, one board president told me that he gets a notification to approve every payment over $1,000. There might be smaller buildings where $1,000 is significant and should go through the approval process, but in this board president's large building, it is not. He has asked the property manager to increase the approval limit to $10,000, but the PM has been slow making this change.

Another client's building had a change in the property management team: same firm, but a different manager and team. With the old management team, our company got paid almost as soon as we sent an invoice. With the new management team, we need to send several reminders before we get paid. Since we, like most businesses, add late fees to outstanding invoices, this delay is actually costing the client more money. This appears to be a breakdown of the internal approval process.

If you or your PM are using a third-party processor, that's fine. Just make sure the right support processes are in place and that you are getting your money's worth.

MONTHLY REPORTS

Every month, board members (but not owners) receive a financial report from their property manager or bookkeeper. This report usually arrives mid-month and the package includes a monthly financial statement, invoices, and bank reconciliations. Usually these reports are provided on a cash basis, so that you can see what money actually went in and out during the month. (By comparison, annual reports are usually provided on an accrual basis. See the next section.)

It is not unusual for financial packages from property management firms to be 150 pages long. They typically list every expense line item with the corresponding invoices; they include the association's bank statements; and they also often have a list of the owners who are in arrears. Because of the in-depth scope of this monthly package, you can imagine how many board members study them carefully (not many!). But these lengthy statements are what we at The Folson Group use to find opportunities to reduce operating expenses. We highly recommend that boards schedule their monthly meetings so that they get their monthly financial package with enough time to review it before they meet.

Property management firms manage multiple buildings, so bookkeeping departments get pretty busy when bank statements come out at month-end, and before the cloud and increased automation it was harder for property managers to meet set deadlines. But today you can usually just ask the property manager to provide your financial statements before your monthly board meeting on the second Wednesday of every month. Like everything else in life, asking nicely goes a long way.

If you are not receiving a monthly financial package or are not receiving it timely, that's a sign that it is time to change property management firms. In today's cloud-based world, there is no excuse for boards not to receive this information on a timely basis.

AUDITED FINANCIAL STATEMENTS

Many associations' bylaws state that the association's financial statements must be audited by a CPA on an annual basis. Following generally accepted accounting practices (known as GAAP), the financial statements are provided on an accrual basis. In accrual accounting, revenues and expenses are recorded when they are incurred, not when the money actually changes hands. (It's not essential to understand accrual accounting in depth for our purposes, but compare this to cash accounting, in which transactions are recorded when the cash actually changes hands. Cash accounting is often used for monthly financial reports.)

The audited financial statements must be distributed to owners within ninety days of the building's fiscal year-end.

THE FINANCIAL STATEMENTS

There are three main financial statements you are likely to see: the balance sheet, the income statement, and the cash flow statement. The *balance sheet* shows you what the corporation holds in assets and owes in debt. The *income statement*, also known in business as the *profit and loss statement*, or *P&L*, shows all the revenue coming in and the expenses going out. The *cash flow statement* shows the cash going in and out from operations, investments, and financing. (To be honest, the cash flow statement is usually pretty confusing for most people, so you may find it less useful than the other two statements.) The audited statements will have notes from the auditor.

THE NOTES

The first time I looked at the audited financial statements of our co-op, I could not make sense of them at all. I am a business analyst who has been analyzing financial statements in SEC filings for decades. If I couldn't make sense of them, how could owners who didn't have a financial background? The memo that everything should be written for an eight-year-old to understand clearly missed the auditor's desk, so if you find your building's annual audited financial report confusing, you are not alone. What I've learned is that much of the critical information is in the notes.

When I started working on Wall Street, I was fortunate enough to have a fantastic mentor named Steve. When I joined his team, he promised he would teach me everything he knew about investments and investing. I jumped right in and started analyzing financial statements and writing research reports for him and his firm. At first, I thought that the critical part was the company's introductory statement (which I came to learn was really a sales pitch), the income statement, the balance sheet, and the cash flow statement. After I'd been in my new role a few weeks, Steve said, "Did you read the notes? In the notes, you find the good, bad, and ugly." That stuck with me, and to this day I still start by reading the notes.

The problem with co-ops and condos is that the notes are often insufficient. Publicly traded companies are legally required to disclose everything in the notes, so they have accountants and attorneys spending many billable hours ensuring all aspects of the business endeavors are disclosed. For a private co-op or condo with maybe a million-dollar budget, not so much. Check your building's last year's audited financials to see for yourself.

It turns out that many auditors use the same notes they have been using since the building was converted, often in the 1980s. If you look at the audited financials for your co-op or condo from ten years ago, I'd hazard a guess that the auditors have pretty much copied and pasted everything except the numbers from year to year. Copy-and-paste makes sense if nothing has changed, but things do change and best practices get revised.

THINGS TO WATCH FOR

Let me give you a few specific things to look for in the financials and the notes. If they are not there or are improperly addressed, talk to your CPA and bookkeeper and get them fixed.

Capital expenses. One frequently omitted note (and a huge miss in my opinion) is a list of capital expenses by year. As an owner, you can add your share of the building's capital improvement expenses to your own individual apartment cost basis to minimize your gains tax when selling. If you don't have this information, when you sell you will pay more in gains taxes than needed. Or you'll have to contact the property manager to get the information, and then the property manager will go to the auditor for it. Wouldn't it make more sense for this to be readily available in the financials in the first place? And from a buyer's perspective, wouldn't it be good to know (1) that the building has this information handy for when you sell and (2) what the building has spent in recent history so you know what to expect?

If you are on the board, you can volunteer to be the person who speaks with the auditor about adding the capital expenses to the notes. If you are an owner but not on the board, ask the board if they would like help with this and volunteer to be the person who writes it up for them to pass along to the auditor.

Combining expenses inappropriately. In reviewing our clients' financials, we often see unrelated expenses lumped together in the same line item. This is just bad accounting, as well as nonsensical. Common problem areas:

- Real estate taxes combined with insurance. Even if you are not a financial wiz, does lumping together a $1 million expense with an unrelated $100,000 cost make sense to you? Probably not, especially if one is half of the budget and the two items are unrelated.
- Water and sewer combined with taxes. Technically, water and sewer could be viewed as a tax since the local city or town imposes it; however, it behaves like a utility, and the dollar amount increases or decreases with the amount used. It is much more logical to have water and sewer listed as a line item subcategorized under utilities.

- All energy and utilities lumped together. In my opinion, electricity, heating fuel, water, and any similar utilities ought to be itemized on the income statement, not in the notes. Especially when sustainability is top of mind, these items should be visible and analyzable.

One final note: Financial statements can be confusing at the best of times. You may find it useful to have someone on your board who is a CPA, CFO, or bookkeeper—someone who plays a financial role in their professional life. That person can help explain things to the rest of the board and ask questions of the auditor in a knowledgeable fashion.

FINANCING CAPITAL PROJECTS

Most buildings' budgets are insufficient to cover the number of large repairs or new construction projects needed. There are several ways to finance capital projects.

INCREASED MONTHLY CHARGES

As you know, apartment owners pay monthly fees (common charges for condos and maintenance fees for co-ops) to cover the cost of shared expenses. Increasing owners' monthly charges is one of the most challenging decisions boards face. Writing that annual letter informing owners that their fees are increasing another 5 percent for the tenth year in a row is never easy. And the impact of an increase in fees can be a decrease in property values (having to pay more every month makes ownership less appealing).

We recently received a call from an owner whose maintenance fees had increased by 50 percent over the prior four years. He felt he needed to sell, as he couldn't afford to stay if these increases continued. My concern came from the fact that such high increases had occurred over such a short period of time, during a noninflationary period. As nonprofit entities, co-ops and condos are expected to break even, not make a profit. There are times when it is appropriate to increase monthly fees, but clearly there was something amiss here, and I felt the vendors should be reviewed and the reason for the increases explained.

ASSESSMENTS

Assessments are temporary charges with a specific end date. They provide an attractive option for paying for capital projects, and they increase the cost basis when you sell your apartment (which lowers your capital gains tax). Assessments should be itemized by the board's CPA, by year, in the annual audited financial statements, as noted earlier. However, assessments can be very large, especially if needed work has been deferred, and with half of all Americans living paycheck to paycheck, caution is encouraged. In the case of Champlain Towers South, the $15 million planned assessment translated to an average of more than $110,000 per apartment, a bitter pill to swallow.

BANK OR LENDER FINANCING

Many financing options (loans) are available for capital projects and energy efficiency upgrades. Banks don't typically lend for capital projects in co-ops (if they do, it may be restricted by the underlying mortgage lender), but they do for condos. When banks don't lend, some alternative lenders can provide short-term financing guaranteed by assessments. With a loan, you avoid the high upfront costs that you face with an assessment, but the tradeoff is that you carry more debt and the total cost of your project increases as a result.

TRANSFER FEES

Transfer fees, or *sales fees*, are fees commonly imposed on buyers or sellers in New York City co-ops and condos upon sale of an apartment. These fees are an alternative means to raise capital for capital projects and maintenance repairs, thus alleviating the need for assessments. The amounts of transfer fees, their structure, and how they can be changed are generally determined by the bylaws.

Here are some ways that the transfer fees can be structured:
- A flat fee
- Dollar amount per share or percent ownership
- Percent of the sales price
- Percent of the net profit
- A high percent in the first year(s) followed by a sliding scale in order to discourage flippers and encourage long-term residency

You may hear transfer fees referred to colloquially as "flip taxes." However, let's be clear that they are not taxes, since they are imposed by the co-op or condo, not by the government. But the catchy name has stuck.

Table 4 summarizes the capital financing options we've discussed.

Table 4: Summary of Capital Financing Options

Financing Approach	Pros	Cons
Monthly fees	Easiest to implement	Has no end date; negatively affects property values
Assessment	Has an end date and offsets cost basis to reduce gains tax when selling the apartment	High initial out-of-pocket cost for owners
Financing through financial institution	Low out-of-pocket cost, can avoid increases	Increases your debt and the total cost of the project
Transfer fees	Helps avoid the need for assessments and loans; can encourage long-term residency	May be a turnoff to buyers

LOOKING FOR COST-EFFECTIVE SOLUTIONS

One of the biggest problems with assessing owners for capital projects is that it can be difficult to get everyone to agree on (1) what needs to be done and (2) how much it should cost. This can cause delays in getting the project started and can result in higher costs than originally planned. A related issue is that some people may not be able to afford the assessment, which could cause them to lose their home. It's critical to do your due diligence in looking for cost-effective solutions and in looking for ways to save money on operational expenses so you have more funds freed up for capital projects when needed.

We once consulted with a board that had been talking for

years about wanting a gym but could not come to a decision. They had one lone proposal presented to them that came with a $250,000 price tag. We provided an alternative with the same scope and quality of equipment for half the price. Based on our suggested membership fee structure, we were able to demonstrate that the gym would pay for itself in less than five years, after which point all collected membership fees would be added revenue for the building.

Let's look at a few more areas where there is often opportunity for savings.

ELEVATORS

A client of ours was replacing their elevators. Their managing agent had provided bids via a dedicated elevator consultant who issued a request for proposals (RFP) and used an industry-standard sealed-bid process. The lowest of the solicited bids came with a steep price tag of $750,000. Our client came to us with the goal of reducing that amount to something more manageable for them. We brought in our professionals to give their opinion and revise the scope to remove redundancies. We worked directly with the consultant and elevator company, renegotiated the same scope, with the same vendor, and successfully cut that price by 33 percent, a savings of $250,000!

The benefit of engaging an elevator consultant is that the consultant handles the bidding and comparison process. On top of that, my firm, The Folson Group, renegotiates those proposals (which is an especially useful thing if board members are uncomfortable engaging in the negotiation process). When we asked this vendor why they didn't make the recommendations we did (which they agreed did not diminish the job in any way) and price the project at the lower price to begin with, their response was basically that no one had asked!

CUSTODIAL SERVICES

Upon our recommendation, one board agreed to cancel the contract for their marble polishing service. The building's staff of twenty-two would be taking over this task, resulting in an annual savings of $36,000. The super was in favor of the arrangement and agreed that the team had plenty of time to perform this additional work. (We often find that one particular staff member will take ownership of a particular task or project and be quite proud of their work and contribution. This should be encouraged!)

We brought in the company that sold the machines (which cost about $2,800) and the marble polishing supplies to train the super and the staff, but after the training was completed and the super and staff were ready to begin, two board members somehow convinced the majority of the board that it was better to keep things as they were. The cost-saving opportunity was lost. Imagine what the building could have done with $36,000 per year.

INSURANCE

Insurance is an area in which premiums can vary wildly for the same coverage from comparable high-quality insurers. We gave one board a quote that would cut their premium by $100,000 per year and yet the board decided to renew their insurance plan with their current insurance broker. Even though we explained that our proposal would result in $1 million in savings over the next ten years, they chose not to make the change. We pointed out that this decision violated their fiduciary responsibility to the owners, but they still did not accept our recommendation.

PHONE SERVICE AND OTHER SMALLER LINE ITEMS

While a building's telephone service accounts for a relatively small fraction of its overall expenses, every dollar counts. When we are consulted to analyze a building's expenses, we have the benefit of comparing them to the hundreds of line items and dozens of data points we have benchmarked in our proprietary database.

In one case, we determined that our client's telephone expenses were much higher than they should have been. After some investigation, we discovered a number of accounts and bills that didn't make sense. Buildings can have direct lines to the door attendant, the super, the concierge, the mechanical room, and so on, but no one at this building could produce a master list of numbers. As I've shared before, I love lists(!!), so we put together a list of all the phone lines the building was being billed for and dialed them one by one. We quickly learned that several numbers weren't even in use. We identified which lines they needed and which could be canceled, and then renegotiated how much they would pay for the remaining lines. In the end, we were able to reduce their monthly telephone expenses by over 60 percent.

When you apply this same approach across multiple expense line items, the savings are often quite significant.

REMINDER: YOUR FIDUCIARY DUTY

When a board is faced with the difficult decision to embark on a costly repair project, they must weigh many competing factors. Addressing a dire threat to safety often comes at a high price. The board at Champlain Towers South knew this all too well as they grappled with the prospect of a $15 million remedial program. As a co-op or condo board member, how do you make the right decision on behalf of your community and neighbors?

Co-op and condo boards have a fiduciary duty to manage the association's finances prudently. This means that board members must make decisions in the best interest of the association and its members, and not for personal gain. They must carefully consider all financial options and make decisions based on what will most benefit the association in the long run. This fiduciary duty extends to all aspects of financial management, from budgeting and investment decisions to prioritizing safety-related capital projects to choosing the right insurance coverage. The board must always act in good faith and with the best interest of the association in mind. Failure to do so could result in personal liability for board members.

CHAPTER 8

QUALITY OF LIFE

*"If we are to live together in peace,
we must come to know each other better."*

—Lyndon Johnson

THERE ARE MANY unique benefits to living in a co-op or condo. In New York City and other large metropolitan areas, many buildings offer proximity to a business district and easy access to restaurants, entertainment, museums, and other attractions. The opportunity for residents to enjoy a wide range of amenities—gym, pool, rooftop garden—more affordably than in a single-family home is also attractive, as is not having to mow the lawn, clean the gutters, repair the fence, or take out the garbage. If you are fortunate enough to live in a nicely maintained, well-run building, with neighbors who are considerate, kind, and engaged in making the building the best it can be, then you likely don't need convincing: co-op and condo living can offer the best of many worlds.

In the previous two chapters, we discussed the safety of buildings and the financial implications of investing in a co-op or condo unit. Perhaps less tangible, and certainly harder to measure, is the satisfaction you feel with the place you've chosen and the quality of life you experience there.

QUALITY OF STAFF

One of the things that can help or hurt quality of life in a co-op or condo building is the quality of the staff running it.

As a resident, the super or resident manager is one of the most important people to get to know. As stated before, we find the super to be the person who can make or break a building, and they have a big influence on the rest of the building staff. When visiting an open house before buying, it's always good to "bump into" a couple of residents in the elevator or lobby and ask them about the super and the staff. Speaking with the doorman when you arrive is another way to get a good feel of how welcoming the building is. They might not want to spill the beans, but it's worth asking how they like working there and what they think of the super and other staff members—how well do they work as a team?

As you know, the property manager runs the day-to-day operation of the building and reports to the board. As a resident you may have less direct contact with the PM than you do with the super, but you will feel their influence nonetheless. And as a board member, your relationship with the PM is critical. If the board receives owner complaints about the property manager, it's always a good idea to hear them out, as ignoring owners can create much bigger problems. If the board decides to change the property manager, it's usually easiest to stay with the same firm and just get another PM.

Finally, the friendliness of the doormen is something that make many New Yorkers feel welcome. Doormen are the first impression of how welcome (or not) residents and visitors feel when entering the building, whether they are coming home from work, waiting for their real estate broker in the lobby, or just passing through. A friendly face and smile can make a real estate deal happen (assuming the apartment itself is as promised in the listing and has more than a closet for a kitchen). And what could be better than coming home after a long day to someone who welcomes you with a big smile, a little small talk, and some empathy? (And I bet your doorman gives your Fido more snacks than you do yourself, as that seems to be the secret weapon for doormen to get the pups to love them.)

GETTING TO KNOW YOUR NEIGHBORS

While having great building staff is important, another factor influencing your quality of life is of course the relationship you have with your neighbors. When a large group of people come together from diverse backgrounds, with varied experiences and different personalities, there exists great potential for them to combine their talents and efforts to achieve a shared mission. This is certainly true for the owners and board members living in a co-op or condo. The question is: how do you begin forging those connections?

In my opinion, the best place to start is simply getting to know your neighbors. I understand that for many people, talking to strangers is not easy. I remember having a pit in my stomach when I started networking many years ago. It felt as though I was walking into a room of strangers. Over time, I realized that just switching my attitude from glass half-empty to glass half-full helped me see that I was walking into a room full of future friends.

I spoke with my friend Joe Apfelbaum, who is a LinkedIn trainer, speaker, author, and networking expert. Joe literally wrote the book on networking! *High Energy Networking* is by far the best networking book I have ever read. In it, Joe tells the story of his journey going from not knowing how to network to becoming a master at it. If you struggle to get out of your comfort zone, you may find the book helpful as well.

I often hear residents in apartment buildings say that they don't want to get to know their neighbors. They speak with people all day long at work, so when they come home, they want to be left alone. It's understandable that many people enjoy their privacy, but in our conversation, Joe and I discussed how residents can go about getting to know their neighbors and the sense of connection and community this can bring.

Joe suggests that anyone who says they don't want to get to know their neighbors might want to think about what is behind their hesitation. Do they have a legitimate fear of interacting with people in general, or is it that they just don't want to know their neighbors? Sometimes proximity to others who may become familiar with your social life and daily routines can be a vulnerable feeling.

According to Joe, the universe puts you next to people for a reason. If you're in an elevator with someone, it's nice to make small talk. Often what you'll find is that if you're friendly to others, the right people will be friendly in return. You don't have to ask personal questions, and you don't have to be the *yenta* of your town, but you just get to know them a little bit.

When I asked Joe if he had any advice for introverts, his answer was intriguing. He said the difference between introverts and extroverts has less to do with how outgoing or social a person is and more to do with how they recharge their energy, whether that's in solitude (introvert) or surrounded by others (extrovert). There are plenty of introverts who are happy to be social and connect with people, but it takes a lot of energy, so they need alone time afterwards to recover. So, introverts, if hundreds of people live in your building, don't feel obligated to get to know everyone. Start with one or two neighbors; even just a greeting can begin to build a relationship.

Building relationships happens over time and requires a bit of risk taking. The risk of greeting strangers, even if they are your neighbors, is that they might not return your greeting. They may not remember your name the next time you see them, or they may be unfriendly or even rude. But when you meet someone who is open to talking and building rapport, the feeling is tremendous. Who doesn't enjoy being called by name the next time they run into a new acquaintance?

After some time, you develop friends, and then the friends turn into a community, and that can be very fulfilling. Many people find that relationships are the most fulfilling aspect of life, so why wouldn't you want to develop those relationships with people you live around? Knowing your neighbors will increase your enjoyment—and also make it easier to resolve issues when they arise.

COMMUNITY ENGAGEMENT

I received a call from Mary, a long-term co-op owner in a large building in Manhattan. She told me that she had had issues with her board and that she now wanted to get involved and run for the board herself. She didn't know where to start, so she decided to reach out to me after reading one of my many posts on LinkedIn. I asked Mary if she could gather together a group of owners, to which she replied that she didn't know anyone in the building.

This made me wonder: Does this board intentionally not engage its neighbors? In my opinion, actively engaging owners is a good board practice. As they say, "Teamwork makes the dream work." A community that runs like a business is a well-oiled machine: The residents are the owners, and they elect a board of directors to represent their interests. This board is responsible for the overall management of the community and communicates regularly with the owners. There is a strong sense of pride in being a part of such a well-run community, and everyone plays a vital role in its success. However, creating a community in a co-op or condo building is not always an easy task. Here are a few suggestions to help co-op and condo boards get residents involved and engaged.

ASK OWNERS TO JOIN COMMITTEES

Residents often want to volunteer in areas where they have a personal interest, so ask volunteers to join committees in the areas with which their interest and/or skills align. Typical committees include the garden committee, decorating committee, communications committee, and green/sustainability committee. (Pro tip: Unless they are in the industry, virtually no one is interested in joining the façade repair committee. After real estate taxes, façades are the most significant expense in a New York City apartment building, and most residents are happy to leave façade repairs for the board to deal with.)

SCHEDULE INFORMATION SESSIONS

When you're having a service such as a fitness center or laundry service installed or upgraded, bring in a third-party expert to explain the project. This is an effective way to educate owners and take the burden off the board. Another benefit of this approach is that if there's a problem with the gym equipment or laundry machines, owners know the vendor's name and contact information so they can go there directly instead of taking out their frustrations on the board.

HOLD SOCIAL EVENTS

People love social gatherings. Organize occasional events for residents to mix and mingle and get to know one another. Holidays are always a great time to hold events, as are retirements of beloved staff members. Parties can be as simple as wine and cheese in the lobby or ice cream on the rooftop.

Social events let neighbors get to know each other on a different level. Many people say hello in the elevators or lobby, but frequently don't know each other's names. At an event, it's so much easier to introduce yourself to each other. (Pro tip: Make name tags available!) As Joe said, the first step is to know someone's name. The next time you meet them in the lobby, saying their name will build connection. Before you know it, you might even become friendly enough to invite them to your apartment for a coffee or dinner. That's a successful community!

Additionally, these types of events offer board members an excellent opportunity to be part of the community and become known by their neighbors as "regular people." We often hear that boards keep to themselves, which is quite understandable since most residents come to them with complaints, not praise. Social events help board members be seen as approachable and likable. Who wants to complain to people they like?

Want to make the time more productive? Have a theme. If sustainability is one of your passions, ask the board if you can hold a "green team" event in the lobby. Gather a few people for a committee, do some research, get some recycling information to share (your city may supply these types of materials upon request), and then have a little table in the lobby to educate people on how to recycle their disposables. (And maybe you could hand out ice cream. I'm just sayin'.)

A social event is also a perfect opportunity for a couple of the board members to give an update about what the board is working on yet keep it informal so that it is quick and doesn't require much preparation. If your board is successful in not needing an increase in owners' fees, what could be better than announcing the good news at the holiday party?

PUBLISH PERIODIC NEWSLETTERS

Proactively update owners on what's going on in the building and what initiatives the board, staff, and property manager are working on. Newsletters are typically quarterly or annual, but some buildings have monthly updates. Some co-ops or condos provide updates only when something negative happens in the building, like an elevator, laundry, or boiler outage. Just as boards should receive praise for a job well done to balance out the many complaints they receive, we recommend including positive updates in the newsletter instead of breaking only bad news.

Although the best practice is for the board to approve the newsletter before distributing it, the newsletter does not have to be written by the board. A group of volunteers can collaborate to create the newsletter and include the super's report from the most recent monthly meeting. An owner with a flair for design can set up an attractive template using a platform such as Canva or MailChimp (both of which have free options). Once the volunteer has the template set up and adds the latest updates to the newsletter, one board member should review and edit it before it's sent to the remaining board members for final approval.

CREATE AN ONLINE COMMUNITY

To facilitate daily communications, consider using an online community platform. You could use a private Facebook group, but there are also platforms designed specifically for building management and communication; among the buildings we have worked with in New York City, BuildingLink is quite popular. These platforms give users a means to communicate, post for-sale items, and list needs or requests such as cleaning services, dog walkers, nannies, and babysitters. A recommendation list for local restaurants, dry cleaners, cobblers, and other small businesses is another popular feature.

COMMON ISSUES AND POSSIBLE SOLUTIONS

Quality of life issues can be challenging to address, in part because residents have differing tolerances and expectations. A classical music fan who hears the faint echo of piano music down the hall will likely have a much different reaction than the pianist's next-door neighbor whose newborn is napping. In fact, noises and smells are some of the most common complaints that we hear from owners. If you have a good relationship with your neighbors, the best place to start is usually talking with them to see if the situation can be resolved. Beyond that, issues often get escalated to the board.

Here are a few common problems and suggestions for handling some of them.

NOISE

When an owner complains about kids bouncing balls or practicing the piano, or TV blasting so loudly that they can't hear their own TV, the primary remedy available to the board is to write a letter to the offending party asking them nicely to keep it down. However, it is possible to write certain guidelines into your house rules as well. For example, your building may have defined "quiet hours."

And in New York City and other large cities, it's not unusual to encounter co-op or condo rules stating that a minimum of 80 percent of the floor in an apartment be covered with carpeting or area rugs to dampen the noise heard by the neighbors below. If your board receives a complaint, it's a good idea to have the PM or super inspect the noisemaker's apartment to double-check that it's mostly covered. (We once had a noisemaker who was wearing stilettos and clomping around at four in the morning above our bedroom. We offered to pay for a wall-to-wall carpet, a proposal they did not accept.)

SMELLS

One lady often cooked salmon and opened her door into the hallway, probably because it was too smelly in her own apartment. But what can a board do about that? It's not like they can tell her she can't have salmon for dinner, and there are no rules against having your door open, so this becomes quite a pickle. (Sorry, I have no good advice here!)

PETS

Poorly behaved pets are a sensitive issue for many people, including pet lovers themselves. We all know that there are some barkers out there, and as they say, you can't teach an old dog new tricks. Including a properly written pet policy in your house rules can help set expectations up front so pet owners understand their responsibility toward their neighbors. For a sample pet policy, see the free downloadable workbook that accompanies this book.

CLEANLINESS

Cleanliness in common areas is something that the super should have under control. When I visit a building, I know to pay particular attention to the basement. A basement that is neat, tidy, and clean demonstrates that the building's super cares about and takes pride in the job and building.

If the board gets complaints about cleanliness, they need to be taken seriously. A lack of attention in this area could also mean a lack of attention to other maintenance issues. Boards can check the building's maintenance log to verify that all the leak and rodent requests have been addressed.

DÉCOR AND AESTHETICS

Preferences in décor are highly personal, so reaching consensus on any aesthetic change to common areas can be a challenge. We once repainted the doors and doorframes from a '90s-era mint green to beige (this was a few years ago when beige was the new black). Some owners got together to protest the change by sending threatening mail to the board. It got so ugly that the board decided to paint sample doors the residents could vote on: one was the old mint green, one beige, and one white. You know what the owners voted for? Beige! This just goes to show how a small but vocal group can make governing a challenge. Although the democratic solution was creative and effective, the time and energy involved could have been better spent on other initiatives.

My best advice for boards is to involve owners in any design and décor changes. Set up a committee to provide input, and allow plenty of time for the committee to argue amongst themselves. And be prepared that even if residents vote, there will likely still be protesters.

PROJECT PRIORITIZATION

Imagine your dream project is to install a yoga studio in the unused roof studio apartment. You're in your Zen zone when you practice yoga. Getting a dedicated practice area would improve your quality of life tremendously.

If you think you need a committee of yoga lovers to accomplish this goal, think again. You may have a neighbor whose questions at the annual meetings are focused on efforts to develop the building's unused spaces to maximize their property value. Another would love to be able to offer her mother a guest room when she comes to visit and suggested the unused apartment as a viable option. Your reasons for wanting to improve your building may differ, but the reason is not essential; the wish and goal are what matter.

The solution here is to organize around the goal by identifying how a project can meet a wide variety of objectives, and recruiting sufficient proponents to support the desired change. My advice to boards is to ask each volunteer who is interested in a project, alone or together with their friends or a committee, to do some research and report back to the board. Ask them to provide a draft plan and a proposed budget that the board can use to make an assessment on whether the project is even feasible. Although it would be extra work for the board, providing a project plan template is a great way to have volunteers and committees provide their ideas in a standardized format.

The bottom line is, getting to know your neighbors and staff not only makes for a friendlier community and better quality of life, it makes your building feel like *home*.

WORKBOOK RESOURCES

Our free downloadable workbook contains:
- Sample Pet Policy
- And more!

To download the workbook, use the QR code below or visit https://www.thefolsongroup.com/book.

CHAPTER 9

SUSTAINABILITY AND ENERGY EFFICIENCY

"Action expresses priorities."

—Mahatma Gandhi

IT IS SAFE TO ASSUME that most co-op and condo owners want to live in a greener, more sustainable building. We would love it if the building that we buy into has a LEED Platinum certification or an energy efficiency grade of "A" according to Energy Star standards. In many of our nation's cities, New York City included, that is not typically the case, but the hope is that we're moving in the right direction. In fact, you can do more than hope. Volunteering for the board or to serve on a "green" committee can enable you to spread awareness and influence future decisions to improve energy efficiency and water conservation in your building.

In Chapter 5, I introduced the benefit of setting SMART goals, goals that are specific, measurable, achievable, results-focused, and time-bound. We set SMART goals for one of our clients to improve their energy efficiency. We determined that, compared to benchmark statistics of similar buildings, this Brooklyn-based condo was using an excessive amount of electricity. One specific, measurable upgrade was to replace all light bulbs with LED bulbs by a particular date. Although lighting accounted for only 20 percent of the building's total electricity usage, the transition to more efficient LED bulbs was specific, measurable, achievable, results-focused, and time-bound.

That 20 percent now runs efficiently, resulting in immediate cost savings. Those savings can be invested in upgrading the remaining 80 percent of electric usage. For example, motion sensors can be installed for the new LED lights in common areas so they turn on only when needed. Lights in the basement would turn on when someone exits from the elevator into the basement, but the majority of the time, they would remain off.

Another measure the board took was encouraging participation from owners inside their apartments. Significant savings can be achieved when owners replace the light bulbs inside their apartments with LED bulbs and seek Energy Star certification when replacing major appliances. Since these apartment-level efforts are voluntary, their success hinges on boards' clear, compelling messaging, and friendly, consistent reminders to owners.

A co-op or condo board is responsible for governing and making decisions that affect the common areas of the building. They can upgrade, retrofit, and make the changes pertaining to their jurisdiction; however, they cannot (for the most part) invade the apartment owners' space. Since the apartments account for the majority of the energy and water use in a building, the board needs the owners' cooperation to achieve optimal energy efficiency and sustainability for the building.

An apartment owner might think, "I pay for my own electricity, so if I want to keep my 75-watt incandescent light bulbs, who is the board to tell me that I should replace them with 8-watt LED bulbs?" This is an understandable privacy issue. However, when it comes to efforts to be green and sustainable, the entire building's usage is counted. In some cities, like New York, penalties can accrue if the building's usage is too high, so individual behavior comes back on the entire community. Therefore, it is in the board's interest to communicate with owners the benefits of replacing wasteful light bulbs and twenty-year-old air conditioners.

While the cause and urgency of climate change are divisive issues for some, most Americans understand the need to improve sustainability. Local governments have passed greenhouse gas emissions regulations, and large corporations have committed their own innovations toward clean air standards within several years. Let's look at some of the laws that affect NYC buildings.

NEW YORK CITY ENERGY LAWS

Under the leadership of Michael Bloomberg, who served as New York City mayor from 2002 to 2013, significant effort was made to reduce greenhouse gas emissions in the city. His administration passed local laws that require large buildings, including residential buildings exceeding 25,000 square feet, to track their energy and water consumption patterns. (Initially, the requirement applied to buildings exceeding 50,000 square feet but was later revised to half that size.) Measuring and benchmarking efforts began so that strategies to improve efficiency could be identified and implemented. An oft-repeated adage in business is "What gets measured gets managed." The corollary, "What doesn't get measured doesn't get done," is applicable to many things in life and business, so these early requirements to track energy use were a laudable start. New York City's current energy-efficiency laws are numerous, but the primary laws that impact most residential buildings include the following:

Local Law 84 (LL84) requires annual benchmarking for energy and water usage using the Energy Star Portfolio Manager for buildings larger than 25,000 square feet. The report must be submitted by May 1 every year, and as long as the filing is completed by the deadline, there is no fine. The most recent report submitted is available on the benchmarking website.

Local Law 87 (LL87) mandates that every ten years buildings larger than 50,000 square feet undergo an energy audit performed by a qualified energy auditor. It also requires that buildings undergo retro-commissioning measures for "base" building systems such as the HVAC, electrical, and hot water systems to ensure optimal operational efficiency—especially important when such systems are dated. Reporting requirements include the submission of an Energy Efficiency Report (EER) by the initial deadline and once every ten years following for the building to meet the retrofit code.

Local Law 95 (LL95) requires that all buildings post their energy efficiency scores near the building entrance. (LL95 of 2019 amended Local Law 33 (LL33) of 2018, which amended the Administrative Code of the City of New York.) An energy efficiency score is the Energy Star rating that a building earns using the United States Environmental Protection Agency's (EPA) online benchmarking tool, Energy Star Portfolio Manager, to compare building energy performance to similar buildings in similar climates.

The letter grade ranges are as follows:
- **A:** Score of 85 or above.
- **B:** Score of 70–84.
- **C:** Score of 55–69.
- **D:** Score of 54 or below.
- **F:** Building did not meet benchmarking requirement deadline.
- **N:** Building is exempt from benchmarking requirement or is not covered by the Energy Star program.

Local Law 97 (LL97) is part of the Climate Mobilization Act of 2019. The end goal is for New York City to be carbon neutral by 2050. The result is a phased program where buildings will be fined for exceeding the carbon emission limit beginning in 2024, with even more stringent emission limits (and thus potentially higher fines for noncompliance) going into effect in 2030. Fines are expected to range from tens of thousands of dollars to hundreds of thousands of dollars annually. Although only approximately 20 percent of buildings are expected to be fined in 2024, the extent of carbon emissions reduction required by 2030 is considerably more ambitious, resulting in the likelihood that 80 percent of New York City buildings will incur fines if they do not reduce their carbon emissions by the deadline.

While some of the NYC laws may seem confusing, they can be grouped into three main categories: measure, shame, and fine.

Measure. Benchmarking was initiated under the Greener, Greater Buildings Plan (GGBP), a 2009 plan started by the Environmental Protection Agency (EPA), and has continued to be a valuable strategy. Any of the laws that require measurement or scoring fall into this category.

Shame. LL95, which requires posting energy efficiency scores, falls into this category. If you have walked down the streets of New York City, you have probably noticed that most buildings now have a "D" posted by their main entrance. (In our estimation, however, it's quite possible that those buildings with an "A," "B," or even a "C" submitted inaccurate or incomplete data.) Additionally, by making reports available online, your building's detailed performance is available for everyone to see.

Fine. The Climate Mobilization Act and the Local Law 97 are bold stabilization plans, proposed with the stated intention of protecting our environment. As noted, the fines they impose will be significant. To avoid them, buildings should complete retrofits by December 31, 2023. We are urging our clients to start planning all retrofits now. (Learn how to engage your co-op and condo neighbors in your building's sustainability efforts by visiting our website and searching for the blog post titled "Energize Your Community.")

ENERGY STAR PORTFOLIO MANAGER

As noted, LL95 requires use of the Energy Star Portfolio Manager, which is a national database and the tool that is used to collect usage data. Utilities companies, including Con Edison (ConEd) in New York, have developed automatic connections with Energy Star. With this arrangement, once an account for a building has been set up in Energy Star and properly connected to the utility, the building's electricity usage can be continuously monitored. Currently there is not a connection showing real-time monitoring of water or heating oil use. With oil being phased out, I doubt that an automatic connection with the oil suppliers will be established. For water usage, I would anticipate that at some point the NYC Department of Environmental Protection will have a similar connection.

I do have one problem with the Energy Star Portfolio Manager, though it's not really with Energy Star; it's with the data being reported. Based on The Folson Group's analysis of the citywide benchmarking data, we suspect that many of those buildings with "A" ratings are not reporting accurate data. Some of the likely discrepancies include:

- **Wrong square footage of the building.** A few years ago, I discovered that in my own building, the listed square footage varied greatly depending on which database you looked at.
- **Wrong age of the building.** My own building, for example, was built in 1957, 1959, or 1961, depending on which database you look at. (The correct answer is 1957.)
- **Wrong number of bedrooms.**
- **Incomplete energy use reported.** Buildings are required to report total energy usage, which includes the energy used in common areas, that used by residents inside their apartments, and that used by retail and commercial spaces, even if they are owned by an outside investor.

For example, a building near us received an "A" grade. This building is heated with natural gas yet reports only 3 percent of its energy use from natural gas. Based on our analysis of the citywide benchmarking data, heating typically accounts for 70 percent of a building's energy use, so this represents a significant departure from what we would expect to see. Coincidentally, cooking gas accounts for 3 percent of a typical building's total energy use. Our conclusion is that this building doesn't report its heating gas at all. With such a glaring omission—whether it was inadvertent or not—it's no surprise the building received an "A" grade.

In a building without commercial spaces, over 60 percent of the energy used is by the residents in the form of heating, hot water, and electricity use. Our opinion is that co-op and condo boards cannot meet New York City's energy efficiency mandates without the help of their residents. In most cases, residents are billed directly for their own electricity usage within their apartment, while their heating and water usage are included in their monthly dues (and therefore are often perceived to be "free"). As a result, getting owners on board and convincing them to take steps toward energy efficiency could prove challenging. The efforts may even be perceived by some as intrusive.

At the same time, residents we speak with hate seeing the "D" every time they enter their lobby. Many residents would do whatever it takes to have it replaced with an "A" or "B" or at least a "C." This is where the board's message to residents is key.

WATER CONSERVATION

Although energy consumption is the biggest challenge when it comes to meeting carbon neutrality, water usage plays a role too, especially when that water is heated.

Replacing wasteful plumbing fixtures with more efficient ones nets the following benefits:

- **Toilet:** Reduces water consumption

- **Showerhead:** Reduces both water and energy consumption
- **Faucet:** Reduces both water and energy consumption

According to the EPA, toilets account for nearly 30 percent of the water usage in the average home, so making sure they operate efficiently can significantly impact a home's total water consumption. In buildings built in the 1970s and 1980s, original toilets can use between 5 and 8 gallons per flush (GPF). Today's standard toilet tank is 1.6 GPF or lower; the State of New York requires new installations to be 1.28 GPF or less. Imagine how much water could be saved if the remaining original toilets in an older building were replaced. Additionally, a leaky toilet, which can waste 200 gallons of water per day, is often the result of an old or worn-out flapper. Replacing an old toilet with a 0.8 GPF vacuum-assisted flapperless toilet provides the most significant reduction in water consumption.

ELECTRICITY FROM SOLAR FARMS

We encourage the boards we consult with to speak with shareholders and owners about the benefits of buying their own electricity from a solar farm, which is a large-scale installation where solar panels collect the sun's energy.

In New York City, the way this works is that ConEd still supplies your electricity; however, ConEd is required to buy an equal amount of electricity from the solar farm that you sign up with. You then receive a 10 percent discount on the energy supply charge. So you get the benefits of renewable energy without having to put solar panels on your roof, and all the charges and credits stay on the same utility bill with service by the same utility company.

For more information, simply search online for the ConEd community solar program. And if you're outside NYC, check with your local power company about renewable energy options.

ELECTRIC VEHICLE (EV) STATIONS

Electric cars are already on the market and electric vehicle (EV) stations are needed. It's time to think about electrifying your parking spaces and garages.

I consider myself a lucky person in so many ways, and one of those is that I have a loving, caring, and all-around wonderful sister, Lotta Fransen. Lotta always sees the good in people and generously makes connections. She is also a master at sales and currently sells EV stations. I spoke to her about my book, and she kindly provided me with some tips on what boards should think about before installing EV stations. (These are, of course, for the lucky few New York City boards who have buildings blessed with parking spaces!)

Two types of electrical currents can be used to fuel an electric car: AC (alternating current) and DC (direct current). An electric car can charge on both AC and DC charging stations, but a hybrid car requires AC charging. There are also variations in the time required to charge different makes of cars.

There are three levels of EV charging stations, as shown in Table 5. Hybrids can charge only on Level 1 stations, which are the ones that plug into a regular 110-volt outlet, while fully electric cars can charge on any of the three stations.

**Table 5: Electric Vehicle Charging Station Levels
(Source: California Energy Commission)**

Level	Uses	1 hour of charge lasts
1 - AC (regular plug)	110 Volt	3.5–6.5 miles
2 - DC (station)	220 Volt	14–35 miles
3 - DC (commercial station)	480 Volt	150–350 miles

Keep these things in mind before installing EV stations:

- It is important to see what the charging needs are. How long are cars parked, and how great a distance do the cars normally travel? In a residential building, the cars are usually parked for at least ten hours at night. Then you need to make an estimate of how many miles the cars drive during the day; we estimate that one kW powers a car to travel approximately four miles.
- If you rebuild the parking lot or garage, add conduits with enough capacity for expansion to the entire lot.
- Carefully plan the locations of the cables so that you can easily scale up the parking lot or garage.
- If you need to secure additional electric capacity, remember to secure enough so that you can easily add to the number of EV stations as needed.
- Charging vehicles is a big energy draw that can cause a system overload. Dynamic load balancing is recommended as a solution that helps charge cars efficiently while still maintaining capacity for other electrical appliances and avoiding overload.
- Consider how you will charge for the electricity. Various payment methods are available, including credit cards, payment apps, and parking apps.

Installing EV stations can help residents who already have electric vehicles, but it also may spur people to make the switch from gas to electric the next time they buy a car—and that's great for the planet!

THE PROFESSIONALS WHO MAKE IT HAPPEN

When it comes to sustainability in residential buildings, there are many professionals involved and alternatives to consider.

The super or resident manager can be instrumental in helping the building run more efficiently. Some energy efficiency upgrades are routinely made by the super and the super's in-house staff, while some larger projects require approval by the board.

Property managers and firms often make recommendations to help the board navigate the complex challenge of improving energy efficiency. The property manager often recommends service providers to give the board direction and support.

In New York City, a residential building or board will engage the services of a mechanical engineer or energy auditor to file the building's LL84 and LL87 reports. Recall LL87 is the retrofit law requiring inspections of the building's energy and water usage systems and identification systems or components that are not functioning at optimal efficiency so they may be repaired or replaced.

Finally, a variety of experts will be engaged depending on the specific project. If your LL87 inspection identified deficiencies, you may need plumbers, electricians, or HVAC specialists. For smaller efforts, such as upgrading all the light fixtures in the common areas to LEDs with motion sensors, you could engage a lighting designer or a mechanical engineer. As with any other service provider, always ask how they price their services to understand the value they bring to the arrangement. And you'll almost always want to get competitive bids before proceeding with any project.

GET CREATIVE AND PLAN AHEAD

When it comes to the pursuit of greater energy efficiency, the common pain point for most boards and residents is that many of the obvious solutions appear to be cost-prohibitive at first blush. Whether it's replacing windows to reduce heat gain and loss or replacing the boiler that heats the building and its water, these projects often require a significant financial investment, extensive planning, and no small amount of inconvenience to residents during installation.

For instance, most buildings in New York City are heated with steam and steam radiators. To replace the boiler and steam system with a more efficient heat pump system would require all new piping to be installed throughout the building. Can you imagine finishing a three-month renovation in your apartment, only to learn from the board that they will soon be ripping through your walls to install new piping? A board that plans far in advance and communicates with residents clearly and often will at least soften the blow of big-ticket upgrades.

Finding the most appropriate solutions requires knowledge, creativity, and imagination, and boards need as much information as possible to make an informed decision on how to invest their own and their neighbors' money. We always start with the easy fixes, the ones that offer a high return on investment (ROI) and are quick and easy to implement. But boards would do well to consult with experts who can advise them on all their options large and small, including opportunities to improve efficiency inside the apartments, in the common areas, and in the basement.

There's no better time to start than today, as every day your building uses more energy or water than it should translates to excess carbon emissions and money lost. Why pay the utility company or pay fines when you could put that money in the pockets of the owners?

THE FOLSON GROUP'S ENERGY EFFICIENCY POLICY

We are out-of-the-box, big-picture thinkers and have developed a proprietary blueprint, The Folson Group's Energy Efficiency Policy©. It is easy for boards to implement, and we believe that it is the most accessible and affordable plan for improving compliance and avoiding future fines as outlined in Local Law 97.

By implementing our energy efficiency policy now, your building will have several years of gradual progress to better gauge whether a costly capital improvement, such as a boiler, window, or roof replacement, is actually needed or can be avoided. The first of our clients to adopt our energy policy has reduced building-wide energy use by approximately 20 percent thus far.

Most buildings turn over 5 to 6 percent of their apartments per year. In theory, this means that about 35 percent of the apartments will be sold in the next seven years. Our energy efficiency policy calls for all sellers to upgrade their apartment and replace their appliances with Energy Star–certified appliances prior to selling. If each one of those units uses 25 percent less energy as a result, the overall energy usage that comes from inside residents' apartments will be reduced by about 8 percent (.35 × .25), significantly reducing the risk of fines in 2030. At the very least, the fines will be lower.

At The Folson Group, we are on a mission to make New York City safer, more sustainable, and more affordable—one building at a time. If your building needs help addressing sustainability issues, please don't hesitate to contact us.

CONCLUSION

FOCUS ON THE FUTURE

*"Today is the opportunity to build
the tomorrow you want."*

—Ken Poirot

FOR ALL THE SENTIMENT that accompanies homeownership, the fact remains that the modern residence is expected to provide safe shelter, life-enhancing amenities, and a sound financial investment for the future.

This book opened with an accounting, some twelve months on, of the tragic collapse of the Champlain Towers South building in Surfside, Florida. Champlain Towers South is the epitome of a worst-case scenario, an earnest reminder of how badly things can go when concerns about safety bump up against the very human traits of indecision, procrastination, and the reluctance to spend large sums of money, even if on unavoidable repairs. How can you help prevent loss and tragedy using the knowledge you've gained? And how might you contribute, as an active owner or board member, to the safety, investment value, and overall well-being of your condo or co-op building?

BE PROACTIVE

At Champlain Towers South, the board appears to have been relying on Band-Aid solutions for years, perhaps even decades. When the concrete slab started sagging, it has been reported that they responded by adding pavers to cover up the problem. Champlain Towers South's maintenance manager from the 1990s, William Espinosa, stated that ocean saltwater would make its way into the underground garage, so much so that "pumps never could keep up with it."[7]

Serving on a board comes with fiduciary responsibilities, so making decisions in the interest of cutting costs and protecting owners' investments comes with the job. But financial decisions can never be made in a vacuum; in sacrificing safety by postponing an expensive repair, a board risks losing much more than money.

Like businesses, proactive boards are usually more successful than those that only react to emergencies. According to The Hay Group, people who are actively engaged in any organization are 43 percent more productive than those who are not.

Here are some steps to help become a proactive board:
- **Educate yourself.** Learn about your current systems as well as potential upgrade alternatives.
- **Develop a plan and take ownership.** This can be as simple as creating a spreadsheet list of all systems with installation and end dates, or as complex as a ten-year capital project plan.

---

[7] Sarah Blaskey and Aaron Leibowitz, "Two days before condo collapse, a pool contractor photographed this damage in garage, *Miami Herald*, 25 January 2022 (www.miamiherald.com/news/local/community/miami-dade/miami-beach/article252421658.html).

- **Be solution focused.** Start with small things that are controllable. Work on minor upgrades that have an immediate or significant result so that you can cross that off and go on to the next upgrade.
- **Be accountable.** Get things done. Don't repeatedly table agenda items; this is a bad habit. Make sure to progress with the plan.
- **Use SMART goals.** Set goals that are Specific, Measurable, Achievable, Results-focused, and Time-bound. (Go back to Chapter 5 for a refresher.)

The board is the backbone of any successful co-op or condo. It can make or break it, depending on how diligently board members prepare for future challenges before they arise. Proactive boards educate themselves and anticipate what's ahead so they can prevent a tragedy from happening on their watch.

ENCOURAGE A CULTURE OF TRANSPARENCY AND AWARENESS

The most effective boards create a community that embraces transparency and awareness. Residents and staff alike need to be comfortable talking to board members and raising issues. In Chapters 5 and 8, we talked about ways the board can communicate to and engage with the building residents, and throughout the book we've talked about ways the board interacts with the property manager, super, and other staff. In a nutshell, build good relationships.

It's also important to be aware of the complaints and maintenance requests in the building so that you can proactively address issues before they arise or escalate. We typically arrange for one board member to be copied on all maintenance requests directed to the resident manager and managing agent. This allows for greater transparency and smoother follow-through.

When a resident manager informs the board that a major plumbing upgrade should be made, the board may disagree, dismissing the recommendation as just the resident manager's opinion. However, if they see evidence of how many leaks residents regularly report, they're more likely to act and approve the upgrade. One of our buildings had a former super who had patched up all the leaky pipes with duct tape(!). Quick fixes are never the answer. They ultimately take more time to undo and become costlier in the long run. As soon as the new management team realized the extent of the duct tape fixes, they started a program to replace all pipes as leaks were reported.

Sometimes transparency can be uncomfortable, but it will pay off in the long run.

CREATE GOALS AND A PLAN

As Stephen R. Covey, author of *The 7 Habits of Highly Effective People*, famously advised in his habit number two, we should "begin with the end in mind." As a board member, ask yourself: What is my ultimate desired outcome? Is it a more cost-efficient building, a greener building, more amenities to better compete with the new luxury condos being built, or something else? Or are you pleased with the current state of your building and the yearly rate increase that you pass on to your residents and neighbors? We know of many buildings where the managing agent will say that, regardless of the circumstances, the board should raise maintenance fees every year so that owners will "get used to them going up"! We find this to be unacceptable and a complete contradiction to the way we review our clients' buildings and make our recommendations.

One of the best ways to keep your co-op or condo association on the right track is to have clear goals and a strong plan related to issues such as budgeting, restoring major building systems, and adding new amenities. Setting goals at the beginning of the board-term year is a good practice, as is starting to plan the budget for the coming year as early as the current mid-year.

Most importantly, have a five-year plan for all expected capital improvements of the building's systems. The capital project plan is necessary to set the yearly budget. Determine the major strategic goals you want to reach during the next one to two years; it's too easy to get stuck in the "here and now" and not pay adequate attention to the future. Also, as the entity in charge of making decisions, the board should be sure that it is in sync with management overseeing the day-to-day operations of the building.

Determine what is required by law, what is urgent, what is needed, what would reduce ongoing costs, and what residents want. Then prioritize what all this entails. (Revisit Chapter 5 for the Eisenhower Box.) Most residents want to live in a safe home with an inviting, friendly atmosphere and as many amenities as possible while paying as little as possible. Striking that balance is no easy task, but once you identify the desired "end," then you will know where to begin.

FINAL THOUGHTS

I hope you have found this book to be informative and useful. I would not be surprised to hear that you were already familiar with many of the topics this book touched on.

If you're a board member, perhaps you've found some helpful tips to make your volunteer position more productive and enjoyable. If you are an owner in a co-op or condo building, I hope you will be inspired to run for your board and take an active role in making your building the best it can be. For those who made it this far despite not (yet!) living in a co-op or condo or serving on your board, if you still found something of value in the book, I will consider it a good use of both my time and yours.

Thank you for reading.

I also hope that this is perceived as a compassionate book, especially in regard to the Champlain Towers South tragedy, as making consequential decisions is not as easy as it may appear to outsiders.

My goal was to convey the importance of getting involved, having a say, and prioritizing the safety of your neighbors and your co-op or condo building. When you are ready to roll up your sleeves, here's how to move forward:

- Download the free accompanying workbook, which includes useful samples, checklists, and templates that you are welcome to rename and use for your own purposes. Visit www.thefolsongroup.com/book or use the QR code below.
- Introduce yourself to one neighbor and talk with them about what they would like to see in the building. Keep the conversation upbeat and positive, and consider

whether you might partner with them on some future project.
- Volunteer, nominate yourself, and get involved.

If you have questions, please contact us through our website (www.thefolsongroup.com)—and be sure to mention that you read the book!

ACKNOWLEDGMENTS

It is with great gratitude that I finish this book. I cannot thank enough those who inspired me to write it. I could name everyone I'm grateful for, but as I am fortunate to have many amazing people in my life, that list would probably be longer than the book itself.

Thank you for being a friend, inspiration, contributor, idea-generator, supporter, mentor, or cheerleader to make this project happen. There is no greater feeling than enjoying the journey toward a goal surrounded by those you care about and those who care about you.

Made in United States
North Haven, CT
07 October 2022